The Eucharistic Controversy

of the Eleventh Century

AMS PRESS

NEW YORK

THE CATHOLIC UNIVERSITY OF AMERICA
Studies in Sacred Theology
Second Series
No. 4

THE EUCHARISTIC CONTROVERSY OF THE ELEVENTH CENTURY AGAINST THE BACKGROUND OF PRE-SCHOLASTIC THEOLOGY

A DISSERTATION

Submitted to the Faculty of Sacred Theology of the Catholic University of America in Partial Fulfillment of the Requirements for the Degree of Doctor of Sacred Theology.

by

REV. CHARLES E. SHEEDY, C.S.C.

Priest of the Congregation of Holy Cross

The Catholic University of America Press
Washington, D. C., 1947

Library of Congress Cataloging in Publication Data

Sheedy, Charles Edmund.
   The eucharistic controversy of the eleventh century.

   Reprint of the author's thesis, Catholic University of
America (1947) published by Catholic University of
America Press, Washington, which was issued as no. 4 of
the University's Studies in sacred theology, 2d ser.,
under title: The eucharistic controversy of the eleventh
century against the background of pre-scholastic
theology.
   Bibliography: p.
   Includes index.
   1. Lord's Supper—History—Middle Ages, 600–1500.
I. Title.   II. Series: Catholic University of America.
School of Sacred Theology. Studies in sacred theology:
Second series; no. 4.
BV823.S48   1980   264'.36   78-63179
ISBN 0-404-16197-9

Reprinted from the edition of 1947, Washington, from an
original in the collections of the University of Chicago
Library. Trim size has been altered (original: 13.5 × 22.5
cm). Text area is unchanged.

MANUFACTURED
IN THE UNITED STATES OF AMERICA

Dedicated to my Mother
and
to the memory of my Father

TABLE OF CONTENTS

INTRODUCTION

The purpose of this study is to set forth the contribution made by the principal adversaries of Berengar of Tours to theological method, and to the substance of Eucharistic doctrine as well, through their use of rational arguments to explain and interpret the revealed data concerning the Holy Eucharist. Both Berengar and his opponents knew from the Fathers and pre-scholastic writers that reason had its place in divine science; and at the same time the program of the medieval schools provided them with a philosophical tool: not a finished metaphysic by any means, but a stream of dialectical writings which had its prime origin in the translations and commentaries of Boethius. Pushed to the limit, and made at once the starting point and the court of highest authority in religious inquiry—and this was the procedure of Berengar —dialectics could lead to an exaggerated rationalism which would take all mystery out of the Eucharist and reduce this great doctrine of faith to the level of a truth comprehensible to unaided reason. But properly ordered, and applied not for the determination of the *content of faith,* but for its explanation and defense, the dialectical arguments of the eleventh-century Eucharistic writers provided a bridge between the conservatism of the post-patristic period and the great syntheses of Christian wisdom which were to begin to appear in the twelfth century, and reach their apex in the *Summa theologiae* of Saint Thomas Aquinas.

The problem of the relations between rational speculation and religious belief has engaged men's minds since ancient times, and it has been variously met at every stage of Christian history. In the ninth century, the two orders of knowledge were thoroughly confused; writers made little attempt to distinguish them in their discussion of religious questions. Gradually as the distinction became more clearly marked between the area of purely rational research and that of faith, men began to emphasize either the one or the other, according to individual differences of temperament and spirit. At the extremes, the dialecticians might use logic to explain away the mysteries of religion, while ultra-conservative writers would attempt to suppress all rational inquiry in favor of a supine traditionalism. At the center, the main stream of Catholic tradition has constantly affirmed that there is no opposition between faith and reason, but a perfect harmony: two orders of knowledge, that of reason, which knows natural truths by natural powers, and that of faith, which knows mysteries revealed by God. The harmony which exists between the two orders of knowledge, constantly affirmed by the great writers of every age, received its definitive statement in the great Constitution of the Vatican Council on the Catholic Faith: "The faculty of reason, illuminated by faith, when it seeks assiduously, lovingly, and soberly, can by God's gift attain to some knowledge of the divine mysteries, both by analogy with those things which it knows naturally, and by the connection between the mysteries and with the ultimate end of human life; but it is never able to comprehend these truths as it does those which are its proper object" (*Sess. iii, Cap. 4, DB 1796*).

But that harmony which has always been seen in principle has not always been so successful in the application, and indeed the failure to respect it lies at the root of all heresies. Beyond the particular problems raised in theological disputation there may lie other problems more general and more fundamental, so that the particular issues involved are rather the occasion and the pretext of the conflict than its essential object. This truth, that a particular conflict may conceal a deeper problem, is nowhere more clearly marked than in the Eucharistic controversy of the eleventh century. Berengar and those who wrote against him shared the same patristic data and the same scholastic training. Berengar exaggerated the importance of rational speculation, tried to use it to establish the content of the mystery of the Holy Eucharist, and thus disqualified himself from any appreciation of the truth of the Mystery of Faith. His principal adversaries, however, — Lanfranc, Guitmund of Aversa, and especially Alger of Liége — accepted the mystery as revealed in Scripture and tradition; but also followed Berengar on to his own ground, gave him argument for argument, and were able through the imperfect tool of dialectics to carry further much that had not been developed thoroughly by the Fathers.

Since this study is concerned with theological method as well as substance, it will be useful first to see the background of the protagonists, the pre-scholastic studies in theology and philosophy. Then will follow an analysis of the Eucharistic theology of Berengar and of his Catholic opponents, first, in the light of their theological principles, their theory of religious knowledge; second, their teaching concerning the doctrine of substantial conversion; and third, concerning the Eucharist as sacrament. We shall see in Berengar false principles leading inevitably to erroneous conclusions. We shall see in his orthodox opponents, on the other hand, important contributions to a clearer understanding of the nature of the Eucharistic conversion, the permanence of the species, and the relations between the *sacramentum tantum,* the *res sacramenti,* and the *res-et-sacramentum.* The Berengarian controversy represents not only a long step forward in Eucharistic theology, but a stage in the development of theology itself.

For their generosity and confidence in permitting him to pursue graduate studies in Theology at the Catholic University of America, the author wishes to express his filial gratitude to his major superiors in the Congregation of Holy Cross, especially to the Very Reverend Thomas A. Steiner, C.S.C., Provincial. He is also grateful to the Superior at Holy Cross College, Washington, the Reverend Bernard Ransing, C.S.C., S.T.D., and to his fellow priests and religious there, especially the Reverend Joseph A. McCartney, C.S.C., for their help and support during many happy months. The Reverend Eugene Burke, C.S.P., S.T.D., Professor of Sacred Theology at the Catholic University of America, under whose direction this dissertation was written, was always patient, generous with his time, and extremely helpful. The librarian of the Andover Theological College of Harvard University was kind enough to lend the author, through the Interlibrary Loan, their copy of Berengar's *De sacra coena,* the only copy of this rare book listed in the Union Catalogue as being in the United States.

To these persons and to all of his friends who helped in other ways, the author wishes to express his thanks and a promise of his daily remembrance in the Holy Mass.

Notre Dame, Indiana.
Feast of Sts. Philip and James, 1947.

CHAPTER I

INTELLECTUAL LIFE IN THE PRE-SCHOLASTIC PERIOD.

The period called pre-scholastic extends from the age of Charlemagne to the appearance of the first scholastic syntheses in the twelfth century.[1] It begins with one renaissance, the Carolingian, and ends in another, "the renaissance of the twelfth century." Between the two extremes intervened a period of decline, the tenth century, "century of iron," perhaps the darkest age in European history; but the Carolingian revival retained sufficient momentum to carry through and make of the second renaissance a continuation and completion of the first.

Politically, this age saw the emergence of the medieval commonwealth from the confusion of barbarism.[2] Intellectually, it was extremely conservative, a period of compilation and reproductions, of great dependence on the teachers of the patristic age. But at the same time an element of progress could be seen in the gradual adaptation of the Aristotelian dialectic to the study of revealed truth, a work of an intellectual *élite,* having its roots in the Carolingian schools.[3] Throughout the pre-scholastic centuries the scholars had access to a stream of dialectical writings which they began to use for the development, understanding, and comprehension of the body of writings which they had inherited from the Fathers.[4]

Thus in these centuries the elements of scholasticism were prepared, and the spirit which was to animate it formed. Before the end of the period a proper place would be assigned to the two factors which were to become predominant in the elaboration of twelfth century synthetic

---

1 B. Haureau, *Histoire de la philosophie scholastique,* Paris, 1872, pp. 40-41. "There were only two different stages in the scholastic period: the first beginning with Alcuin and ending in the twelfth century, the second beginning with the thirteenth century and ending at about the time of John Gerson."

2 C. Dawson, *The Making of Europe,* New York (Sheed and Ward), 1934, Chap. 12, "The Restoration of the Western Empire and Carolingian Renaissance," pp. 214-233.

3 J. De Ghellinck, *Le mouvement théologique du XIIe siècle, Études, Recherches, et Documents,* Paris, 1914, Chap. 1, "La préparation théologique du XIIe siècle," pp. 1-66.

4 M. Grabmann, *Die Geschichte der Scholastischen Methode,* Vol. 1, Freiburg-im-Breisgau, 1909, p. 189.

1

works, especially the epochal manual of Peter Lombard. The first of these two elements, a respect for traditional texts, was to owe much to the Carolingian institutions; and the second, a dialectical finesse, was the achievement of the pre-scholastic schools.[5]

1. *The Conservative Element: The Study of the Sacred Page*

The decline of western theology which took place immediately after the death of St. Augustine in 430 was largely due to the vast political and social upheavals which accompanied the invasions. As early as the second century after Christ, the tribes of the outer lands were in movement, and forces were being gathered which could only find outlet in violent explosion. The storm burst in the third century: the Empire, weakened by civil war and continual mutinies, was attacked on every frontier; and Europe became the scene of a momentous struggle between the dying Empire and the fresh vigor of the barbarian hordes.[6] In 378, at Adrianople, the Gothic cavalrymen won a decisive victory over the Roman infantry under Valens.[7] Alaric, the Visigoth, sacked Rome in 419;[8] wave after wave of invaders rolled over the west. During the fifth century, Burgundians, Visigoths, and Franks were in Gaul;[9] Vandals, Suevi, Alans, and Visigoths- overran Spain;[10] and the Saxons invaded Britain, already weakened by the withdrawal of the legions which had taken place in 426.[11] In 429, The Vandals under Gaiseric evacuated southern Spain to attack North Africa.[12] In the following year, when St. Augustine lay dying at Hippo, the invaders were at the city's gates, and within ten years the Vandals had become masters of Africa.[13] To conclude this brief sketch of the upheavals of only one century, in 476 Odovaker exiled the last nominal emperor, whose name, ironically, was Romulus, and finally Theodoric the Ostrogoth set up a kingdom in Italy in 493 and restored some order to the west.

---

5 De Ghellinck, *op. cit.*, p. 6.

6 Dawson, *op. cit.*, pp. 75-77.

7 *Ibid.*, p. 87.

8 *The Cambridge Medieval History* (H. M. Gwatkin and J. P. Whitney, edd.), vol. 1, "The Christian Roman Empire and the Foundation of the Teutonic Kingdoms," New York, 1911, p. 273.

9 *Ibid.*, pp. 277-303.

10 *Ibid.*, p. 304.

11 *Ibid.*, pp. 380-381.

12 *Ibid.*, p. 305.

13 *Ibid.*, pp. 306-307.

It would be an exaggeration to set up the history of the invasions as a story of complete and utter social disaster, since out of the maelstrom was formed a vigorous Europe which exerted a world wide political and cultural supremacy for many hundreds of years, a hegemony which it has not even yet entirely lost. Nor were the invasions entirely disastrous to the Catholic faith. In the midst of the convulsions, the faith was preserved, and even extended; religious unity continued to hold together the various members of that large family which the barbarians divided among themselves.[14]

But from the viewpoint of religion, the age of the invasions was a time for missionary work, not for the development of theology. "It is easy to see," as Tixeront has pointed out, "that serene contemplation and pure speculation cannot thrive in times such as these. . . . During these ages and in these circumstances, it was no small merit to preserve the traditions of the past and inculcate the rudiments of religious doctrine in the unruly neophytes who were then entering the Church."[15]

Consequently, the sacred doctrine of these ages of invasion took the form of a practical and simple summary of the teachings which had been elaborated by the Fathers and theologians of earlier times.[16] Two great names stand out, that of St. Leo (†461) and St. Gregory (†604), both of them popes and Fathers of the Church, both deservedly surnamed "the Great." St. Leo, the more original of the two, is one of the most profound doctors of the Incarnation, while St. Gregory adapted the teaching of St. Augustine to the practical needs of religion in his day.[17]

Apart from St. Leo, then, the writers of the pre-Carolingian theology lack originality and individuality. They felt they could not add to nor improve the work which had been done, and confined themselves to collecting texts. The great men of this period, not to mention mere copyists, are Boethius, Cassiodorus, St. Leo, St. Isidore of Seville, St. Gregory the Great, Julian of Toledo, and the Venerable Bede.[18] Boethius and Cassiodorus were to have great influence in the formation of western theology, but their influence was not in the field of sacred doctrine precisely, and they were not official teachers.

---

14 J. Tixeront, *History of Dogmas*, tr. from the 5th French edition by H. L. B., St. Louis, 1916, vol. 3, p. 305.
15 *Ibid.*, pp. 305, 312.
16 *Ibid.*, p. 305.
17 *Ibid.*, p. 306.
18 De Ghellinck, *op. cit.*, p. 4.

The Carolingian age, extending from Charlemagne's accession as sole ruler of the Franks in 771, until the dissolution of the Empire in 887, has justly been termed a "renaissance," but it would be a mistake to think that during this century there took place any marked advance in the teaching of theology. Indeed, throughout the ninth century, and the tenth and eleventh as well, theological teaching was characterized by the notes which we have marked in the preceding age, traditionalism and dependence; and the intellectual progress which was doubtless made took place in another quarter, the *trivium* and *quadrivium* of the schools.

When we speak of "theology" during the Carolingian age we ought not to think of a program of studies and a method of teaching such as were to be offered by the universities of the thirteenth century. Even the word "theology" was not to acquire its present meaning until the twelfth century. Throughout the period which we have been discussing, the term used to designate the sacred studies was "Pagina Sacra." Towards the end of the eleventh century "quaestiones sacrae paginae" began to appear, but it remained for Abelard to give us the term as we understand it today: rational speculation concerning revealed data. Even St. Thomas will adhere to an older terminology and will designate Christian teaching under the term "De sacra doctrina."[19]

And in the age of Charlemagne, theological teaching, in the sense of an orderly system of studies preceded by philosophy, simply did not exist. Charlemagne issued many capitularies for the instruction of the clergy, but the emphasis was on liturgical correctness, not on speculation. Priests were required to know the Athanasian and Apostles' Creed; they should know the Lord's Prayer and be able to explain it; they should know how to say Mass and apply the penitential discipline. No higher ideal of literacy was demanded of them than that they be able to write letters.[20] For preaching, they had some translations into the vernacular of certain patristic homilies, and their library was limited to some biblical and liturgical works, a collection of canons, the penitential, and some writings of the orthodox Fathers, especially the homi-

---

19 For the use of the term "theology" in the pre-scholastic times, see G. Paré, A. Brunet, P. Tremblay, *La rénaissance du XIIe siècle, les écoles et l'enseignement,* Paris and Ottawa, 1933, pp. 307-309. This valuable work is a complete revision of the work of G. Robert, *Les écoles et l'enseignement de la théologie pendant la prèmiere moitié du XIIe siècle,* Paris, 1909. Cf. De Ghellinck, *op. cit.,* Appendix A, p. 66, and J. H. Newman, *Historical Sketches,* vol. 2, London, 1903, p. 475.

20 Charlemagne, *Capitula de doctrina clericorum* (yr. 802), MGH (Legum) 1: 107; also in PL 94: 249.

lies of St. Gregory.[21] In the century of iron which followed the dissolution of the Carolingian Empire the program of priestly studies remained what it had been before. As De Ghellinck sums it up, "Study of theology was limited to the reading of the Scriptures and some Fathers, with commentary, and the great care was that priests should know something of the ritual, a knowledge which they had to acquire through their own efforts or under the direction of a bishop or some older priest. There is no question of a metaphysic of dogma, or even of an organic classification of theology, and for a long time it will be so."[22] The Carolingian century had produced at least men of the stature of John the Scot, Paschasius Radbert and Ratramn, and Raban Maur; the succeeding century produced one great scholar, Gerbert, and one important theological work, the treatise on the Eucharist of Heriger of Lobbes, a continuation of the Eucharist discussions begun by Paschasius and Ratramn.[23]

One final aspect of pre-scholastic intellectual life is worthy of comment before passing on to the investigation of its greatest contribution, the program of the schools. This is the collection of texts and the copying of manuscripts, a conservative work in the literal meaning of the word, but of inestimable importance for the formation of scholasticism and of western culture in general. Charlemagne himself was extremely zealous to secure the multiplication of manuscripts and the use of correct texts. Indeed, we owe it to Charlemagne and Alcuin that we are able to *read* medieval manuscripts; they replaced the variety of illegible scripts of the Merovingian age with a new style of writing which became almost standard throughout the western world: the Caroline minuscule, which originated perhaps in the Abbey of Corbie in the second half of the eighth century, and provided the foundation of the style we use today.[24] Through the work of the monastic copyists of the early Middle Ages most of Latin literature was preserved for us, and the foundation was laid for what became and has continued to be the literary tradition of the west.

But the point at which the pre-scholastic period exerted its greatest influence towards the formation of scholasticism was not its rudimen-

---

21 De Ghellinck, *op. cit.*, pp. 14-15.

22 J. De Ghellinck, S.J., "Dialectique, théologie, et dogme au Xe-XIIe siècles," *Beiträge zur Geschichte der Philosophie des Mittelalters,* Festgabe Zum 60. Geburtstag Clemens Bäumker, Münster, (Supplementband, 1913) pp. 79-99.

23 J. De Ghellinck, *Le mouvement théologique* . . . , p. 35.

24 C. Dawson, *op. cit.*, p. 226.

tary program of theology, nor the copying of manuscripts, but the genesis of philosophy which took place in the schools. The application of liberal studies to the understanding of divine revelation was the actual initiation of the program of scholasticism.

2. The Element of Progress: The Dialectics of the Schools

Even during the decline of the western Empire, humanistic studies had flourished, but the march of the barbarian invader put an end to the imperial studies as it did to the tottering Empire itself; and for a long time scholarship on the Italian peninsula was to exist only in isolated refuges, the studio of Boethius, the monastery of Cassiodorus in Calabria, and in the papal court. When learning reappears, it will be farther to the north and in a new setting, the humble cloister replacing the brilliance of the imperial Athenaeum. For two centuries, Ireland was "the one bright spot in the dark night which covered Europe."[25] John the Scot and Clement came to the Frankish school from Ireland, Alcuin from York, and missionary monks from Ireland and England, St. Columba, St. Gall, and St. Boniface, restored studies at Luxeuil, Saint Gall, and Fulda.

The great resurgence of learning in the west took place in the ninth century and had its source and center at the court of Charlemagne and his immediate successors. Charlemagne's original intention, as we have seen, was to improve the intellectual condition of the Frankish clergy; but the accomplishment outstripped the purpose: libraries began to be collected, scholars were imported from England and Ireland, Italy and Spain, and a real revival of intellectual life began to take place.[26] It is true that the Carolingian renaissance, so far as the palace itself was concerned, ended with the dissolution of the Frankish Empire, and was not continued. But Charlemagne insisted on the establishment of schools in the monasteries and cathedrals, and it was in these local centers that intellectual life went on. From the ninth century onward,

---

25 M. De Wulf, *History of Medieval Philosophy*, 3rd. English edition, transl. from 6th. French edition, E. Messenger, London, 1935, vol. 1, p. 50.

26 Cf. G. Brunhes, *La foi chrétienne et la philosophie, au temps de la Rénaissance carolingienne*, Paris, 1903, p. 10. "Doubtless certain elements of culture did not issue from the court of Charlemagne. The monasteries founded in Germany by the disciples of St. Boniface, those of Italy, the contact of Spain with Arabic civilization, and a certain permanence of rudimentary literary culture had prepared the way for a renaissance; but the establishment of a degree of peace, which made it possible to profit from the heritage of the past, and the creation of a current of intellectual activity from which would result the literary renaissance of the west, are due certainly to the personal action of Charlemagne and the churchmen who carried out his designs."

the story of medieval letters is the story of Tours, Fulda, Reichenau, Fleury, Lorsch, and Corbie; of Metz, Cambrai, Rheims, Auxerre, and Chartres — the monastic and cathedral schools.[27]

It is interesting to observe the process by which an institution may gradually enlarge its external scope and influence, all the while remaining true to its inner life and purpose. This process of evolution can be clearly seen in the development of monasticism in the west. The cultivation of letters simply did not enter into the original program of monasticism. As the monastic society was first conceived, a man did not become a monk because he wished to teach or be taught; he became a monk because he was anxious about his soul, and was willing to consecrate his life to God in a more perfect manner in order to be sure of his soul's salvation.[28] "To flee, to be silent, to weep" — the monastery was a haven, a place of refuge, and at the same time a protest against the worldliness of a court Christianity which had fallen from the primitive fervor. The only qualification demanded of an aspirant was that he be truly seeking God. The rule of St. Benedict had nothing to say about schools; not even the copying of books was part of the rule, although it could and did enter into the prescribed program of manual labor.[29] It was not necessary for a monk, unless he was a cleric, to be able to read and write. He did not lecture nor teach; he did not speak at all, except to sing the daily praise of God in choir.

Obviously, the pursuit of studies, especially of profane and liberal sciences, did not enter as primarily important into an institution such as this. But as monasticism developed in the west, almost without knowing it the Benedictine institution began to exercise social and cultural leadership. The basic reason for what may be called this social potentiality in monasticism can be found in the character of the institution itself as St. Benedict adapted it to the west. The great law-giver rejected the

---

27 C. H. Haskins, *The Renaissance of the Twelfth Century*, Cambridge, U.S., 1933, p. 18.

28 Cardinal Newman, *op. cit.*, p. 452, has written luminously concerning this aspect of the monastic spirit. "I remind the reader, if I have not sufficently done so already, that the one object, immediate as well as ultimate, of Benedictine life, as history presents it to us, was to live in purity and die in peace. The monk proposed to himself no great or systematic work, beyond that of saving his soul. What he did more than that was the accident of the hour, spontaneous acts of piety, the sparks of mercy or beneficence, struck off in the heat, as it were, of his solemn religious toil, and done and over almost as soon as they began to be. . . . He cared little for knowledge, even theological, or for success, even though it be religious. It is the character of such a man to be contented, resigned, patient, and incurious; to create or originate nothing; to live by tradition."

29 Haskins, *op. cit.*, p. 34.

eremitical ideal, with its tendency to isolate the monk and insulate him against contact with society, and adopted in its place the ideal of the common life, in which the monastery itself formed a social unit, capable of radiating its influence outside.[30] The monasteries were areas of stability in a social order as yet unformed; men saw the productivity of the monastic life and began to depend on the monks and look to them for guidance and direction. The monk had renounced the world, but found himself responsible for its care.[31]

Moreover, there were elements in the character of the monastic institution which required the rudiments of intellectual life. The nature of monastic life required the possession of certain books: the Sacred Scriptures and the liturgical books for singing in the choir. It must have a school, for clerical novices at least, and some elementary textbooks. A certain number of monks must be able to read and write, to copy charters and title deeds, to keep the register of monks and the necrology. Every monastery needed a calendar of feasts; and the calendar provided a useful framework for those random jottings which became the annals of medieval history. "A library, a school, an archive, the rudiments of a record of its own, these were incidental to the existence of the monastery and formed the nucleus of an intellectual life."[32]

The Carolingian renaissance gave great impetus to these elements already present in the monastic way of life. Gradually the schools were formed, with the studies no longer limited to monastic recruits, but open to externs also.[33] The decreasing emphasis on merely manual labor, the

---

30 Abbot Cuthbert Butler, O.S.B., "Monasticism," *The Cambridge Medieval History*, vol. 1, p. 525: "It was not the least of St. Benedict's contributions to western monachism that he introduced, with the modifications called for by differences of climate and national character, a type of monachism, more akin to the Pachomian, in which work of one kind or another, undertaken for its own sake, forms an essential part of the life."

31 Newman, *op. cit.*, pp. 442-443: "And indeed a greater shock can hardly be fancied than that which would overtake the peaceful inhabitants of the cloister on his finding that, after all, he so intimately depended still upon this moribund world, which he had renounced forever, that the changes which were taking place in its condition were affecting his own. . . . They had retired into deserts, where they could have no enemies but such as fast and prayer could subdue. . . . They had secured some refuge whence they might look around at the sick world in the distance, and see it die. But when that last hour came, it did but frustrate all their hopes, for, instead of an old world at a distance, they found they had a young world close to them. The old order of things died, sure enough; but then a new order took its place, and they themselves, by no will or expectation of their own, were in no small measure responsible for its very life. The lonely Benedictine rose from his knees, and found himself a city." Cf. Haskins, *op. cit.*, p. 33.

32 Haskins, *op. cit.*, p. 36.

33 Paré, Brunet, Tremblay, *op. cit.*, p. 40.

elevation of a greater number of monks to the clerical state, developed the old "lectio" of the rule into a true program of study.[34]

The monastic schools reached their peak in the generation which followed the death of Charlemagne, among the pupils and successors of Alcuin: men such as Einhard, Raban Maur of Fulda, Walafrid Strabo, abbot of Reichenau, Servatus Lupus, abbot of Ferrières — it was through them and men like them that scholarship in the ninth century reached its highest development.[35] The course of studies comprised the liberal arts of Cicero and Varro, divided by Martianus Capella, and after him by Alcuin, into the *trivium* (grammar, rhetoric, dialectic), and the *quadrivium* (arithmetic, geometry, music, and astronomy). The arts course was designed for the formation of the clergy and was considered as preparatory to the study of the "pagina sacra." Thus the purpose of grammar was to enable clerics to read and understand the Bible; rhetoric and dialectic would help them follow the arguments of the Fathers; the course in music would make more beautiful the sacred chant.[36] Even arithmetic had its preparatory role: for a better understanding of the mystic numbers of the Bible.[37]

Towards the end of our period, late in the eleventh century, cultural leadership passed from the monastery to the cathedral. The monastic and cathedral schools are always mentioned together, but they were radically different in their spirit, in their customs, and even sometimes in the studies they inculcated. If the monasteries led the way at the beginning of the pre-scholastic period, the cathedrals far eclipsed them at the end.[38]

There are a number of reasons for this change. One very obvious reason was the rapid growth of cities, which took place at the end of the eleventh and the beginning of the twelfth century. The monasteries were abandoned to their rural isolation, and an intellectual isolation followed.[36] A second reason was the strong eleventh century movement

---

34 *Ibid.*
35 Dawson, *op. cit.*, p. 228.
36 Brunhes, *op. cit.*, p. 17.
37 De Ghellinck, *Le mouvement théologique* . . . , p. 13. Cf. Alcuin, *Epist. 83 ad Carolum Magnum* (yr. 798), PL 100: 272-273.

Note that not *all* the liberal arts were taught in every school; indeed, not every monastery had a school, and in certain monasteries, particularly towards the end of the pre-scholastic period, all secular studies were prohibited. Cf. R. Heurtevent, *Durand de Troarn et les origines de l'hérésie bérengarienne*, Paris, 1912, p. 32. But in a general way, sufficient for a brief survey such as this, it is true to say that the *trivium* and *quadrivium* represent the pre-scholastic schedule of studies.

38 Paré, etc., *op. cit.*, p. 18.
39 *Ibid.*, p. 40.

for monastic reform. Science and letters do not always go hand in hand with spiritual fervor; indeed, the great monastic reformers regarded studies as an obstacle to the full achievement of the monastic ideal, and strove to eliminate the arts and poetry from the schools. The discipline of the monastery was extremely rigid, not only for the monks in their formation, but also for lay pupils.[40] Meanwhile, the organization of the cathedral chapters around the bishops had provided the secular clergy with a stable centrality of organization similar to that of the monastery, but free from its traditional rigidity. Milder customs grew; pupils could choose their school and masters, and certain of the masters, Fulbert, for example, at Chartres, achieved great reputation. In every way the cathedral schools were more attractive to the independent spirit of the changing times. "The monastic institution and its schools, in the twelfth century, lost contact with the new times; the spirit of initiative and the feeling for progress passed into other hands; its science, at least in a general way, was only a conservative erudition, hostile to dangerous novelties."[41] Citeaux, where extern students were excluded and any but sacred studies proscribed, is far removed from Fulda, Saint Gall, and Reichenau. It is from the cathedral, and not from the monastery, that the renaissance of the twelfth century, the end and the achievement of the pre-scholastic period, will take its rise.

Dialectics was the rational discipline which more than any other was to influence the development of scholasticism. St. Augustine had seen in dialectics a value which lay not merely in subtlety of argumentation but also in the approach to objective truth; and for him, as we shall see in the next chapter, this value extended to the realm of religious truth as well as to that of the things of nature. The pre-scholastic writers knew St. Augustine's estimate of the value of dialectics, and for them the rational approach to truth consisted mainly in the dialectical approach.

But this is not to say that the pre-scholastic philosophy consisted exclusively in a discipline of logic. In the first place, the renaissance of the ninth century was not even exclusively philosophical in nature, but extended to all the branches of learning then known.[42] Alcuin, Servatus Lupus, and Walafrid Strabo were humanists as well versed in Vergil

---

40 Cf. Heurtevent, *op. cit.,* pp. 30-31, for an interesting note on the discipline of the late eleventh century monastic school, taken from the life of St. Anselm.

41 Paré, etc., *op. cit.,* p. 39.

42 De Wulf, *op. cit.,* p. 116.

as in the Fathers and dialectical writers. John the Scot was a scholar of Greek, and in the century following, Notker Labeo was to become a pioneer in the German language and Gerbert of Aurillac was to become famous in mathematics. The scholars of the pre-scholastic age were all monks and churchmen, but they were by no means exclusively concerned with divine science or with the rational explanation of it.

And again, even in their philosophy they were not mere dialecticians. It is true that separate philosophy, as an organized branch of study, as we understand it today, existed only in a gradual and rather scanty dialectical teaching; but it is a false view that this teaching represented the whole of philosophy. "It must not be forgotten that if works of philosophy are rare, the writings of the Fathers and the Scriptures contained a whole philosophy."[43] Instead of limiting the philosophy of the time to logic, we should be more just in saying that in the study of theology, at the school of the Fathers, were found the important questions of philosophy, though not as autonomous branches as we study them today.[44]

Nor was the pre-scholastic philosophy in its ninth century beginnings entirely Aristotelian in its inspiration and content. It seems on the contrary to have been Platonist.[45] The influence of Aristotle depended upon the gradual reception of the various parts of the Aristotelian *corpus,* and even that influence came about indirectly, through translations. The influence of Plato was also indirect: until the twelfth century, only the *Timaeus* was known in the west, in the translation of Boethius, and was exercised chiefly through the mediation of St. Augustine, eagerly seized upon by John the Scot, through whom the first period of the Middle Ages came into contact with the thought of Greek mysticism.[46] But the Platonist influence, with all of its importance in the great philosophical question of universals, did not bear so directly on the formation of scholasticism and the Eucharistic controversies as the dialectics of Aristotle.

Finally, it cannot be said that the pre-scholastic philosophers were entirely without metaphysics. It is true, they possessed neither the *Metaphysics* of Aristotle, nor the *De anima,* nor the *Physics;* they possessed

43 Brunhes, *op. cit.,* p. 15.
44 *Ibid.,* p. 43.
45 *Ibid.,* p. 24.
46 De Wulf, *op. cit.,* p. 135.

only the works on logic, as we shall see. Moreover, Boethius, through whose translations the logic principally came to them, insisted on the verbal side of logic. "The treatise on the predicaments," he wrote, "is concerned with words, not things."[47] But Boethius made no mistake concerning the relation between the words and the things which they signify. Words are signs of really existing things, and the things which are signified by words constitute the *genera of reality*.[48] Grabmann has pointed out that all the important metaphysical doctrines of Aristotle are to be found in germ in Boethius: scattered references to matter and form, change, potentiality and actuality, personality, the four causes, and of course, substance and the nine accidents, the categories of being.[49] One of the major points of this study is that Berengar of Tours approached the Eucharist almost exclusively from the dialectical point of view; but it was not precisely as a dialectician that he went astray: the basic error of Berengar was a false metaphysical principle.

An intellectual culture, then, which was not exclusively philosophical; a philosophy which was not exclusively Aristotelian; an Aristotelianism which was not exclusively dialectical, but contained the seeds of a metaphysic as well — with these qualifications made, it may be safely asserted that the influence of the Aristotelian dialectic was predominant in the development of the scholastic method, and in the rational arguments which entered into the Eucharistic discussions of the eleventh century. If Aristotle did not form entirely the substance of European thought, he was at least responsible for its way of thinking, and in no small part for its substance.[50] And even more specifically, in the pre-scholastic period the influence of Aristotle was largely, almost exclusively, felt in the field of dialectics. Throughout the period, that is, from the beginning of the ninth century till the first quarter of the twelfth, the medieval scholars possessed nothing of Aristotle except the logical works of the *Organon;* and not all of them; and none of them in the original, but only in Latin translations, adaptations, and manuals.[51] It was not until the twelfth century that this slender library was to be

---

47 Boethius, *In categorias Aristotelis,* 1, PL 64: 162 C.

48 *Ibid.,* 161, A, C.

49 *Op. cit.,* p. 158.

50 P. Mandonnet, *Siger de Brabant et l'averroisme latin au XIIIe siècle.* Collectanea Friburgensia, Fasc. 8, Fribourg (Suisse), 1899, p. 22.

51 For detailed information concerning the tradition of Aristotelian dialectic in the early Middle Ages, the reader is referred to an article by A. Van de Vyver, "Les étapes du développement philosophique du Haut Moyen Age," *Revue belge de philologie et d'histoire,* 8 (1929), 425-452.

enriched with the discovery of the second part of the *Organon* and the new metaphysics. Till then, the rational approach to revealed truth must consist in the dialectical approach; in this approach can be seen the beginnings of scholastic theology and the source of the rational arguments which Berengar and his opponents in the eleventh century applied to their study of the revealed doctrine of the Holy Eucharist.

See also De Ghellinck, "Réminiscences de la dialectique de Marius Victorinus dans les conflits théologiques du XIe et du XIIe siècles," Revue neo-scholastique, 18 (1911), 432-435.

On the importance of Aristotle in the formation of western culture, see P. Mandonnet, *Siger de Brabant et l'averroisme latin au XIIIe siècle*, Collectanea Friburgensia, Fasc. 7, Fribourg (Suisse), 1899, pp. 17-23.

On the special importance of Boethius as the prime mediator in the first tradition of Aristotle to the west, see excellent chapters in E. K. Rand, *Founders of the Middle Ages*, pp. 135-180, E. S. Duckett, *Gateway to the Middle Ages*, pp. 147-212, and Grabmann, *Die Geschichte der Scholastischen Methode*, pp. 148-177.

The work of A. Clerval, *Les écoles de Chartres*, Chartres, 1895, is of great value for the study of intellectual life in pre-scholastic times.

CHAPTER II

REASON AND AUTHORITY IN THE PRE-SCHOLASTIC PERIOD

The ninth-century pioneers of scholasticism had at their disposal a twofold intellectual tradition, the older tradition of the sacred page, and the newer teaching of the liberal arts, of which dialectics occupied the summit. It remained for them to bind the new philosophical knowledge to that which was already acquired, and to direct the whole towards intellectual unity. That this unifying ideal failed of an altogether consistent and harmonious achievement is not at all due to any divergence on principle among those who took part in the development, for all agreed on the authority of Scripture and tradition and of the Church, and on the utility of rational speculation in the search for divine truth. But at the same time the pre-scholastic writers were unable to distinguish clearly between the two sources of knowledge, and the inevitable mistakes and puerilities of the "dialecticians" led to an anti-intellectual reaction on the part of those who favored a more conservative traditionalism. Throughout the period the principle of harmony between faith and reason was kept in mind, and controversy resulted only from its misapplication.

It is incorrect, therefore, to set up authority and reason as two conflicting sources of knowledge, as if a man in following authority was compelled to abdicate his reason and in following reason must reject the argument of authority. The object of faith, though not derived from reason, requires the use of reason to express the truths of faith and their relations to each other, and to draw out the conclusions implicitly contained in the revealed principles. During the pre-scholastic centuries the attempt was made to apply reason according to this principle of harmony; and if the attempt issued in large part in theological controversy, it was because ratiocination was still defective and immature.

In this chapter the attempt will be made to sketch briefly the initial efforts which were made to bring the two orders of knowledge into one. First we shall set down the great principle of harmony: the eminence of authority and the value of reason as propaedeutic to divine science. Then we shall attempt to explain that the dialectical controversies of the age resulted either from an entire confusion between the two orders of faith and reason, or from the exaggeration of reason's *role* on the part of certain "speculative" writers. The pre-scholastic philosopher-theologians had no desire to contradict the teachings of the Church, though there were in certain of them tendencies which if exaggerated might lead to heresy. Berengar of Tours was the first to construct of rationalist tendencies the substance of his theology. No theologian before him would have dared, nor would the thought have occured to any of them, to characterize a Council of the Church as a "council of vanity" and "seat of Satan," as he termed the Council held at Rome in 1059.[1]

1. *The Principle of Harmony*

First, then, it must be pointed out that there was unanimous agreement among pre-scholastic writers upon the inspiration and inerrancy of the Scriptures, upon the absolute validity of the argument from tradition, if correctly presented, and upon the final authority of the Church as authoritative interpreter of apostolic doctrine. In these matters, as in many others, it was St. Augustine who provided the framework of medieval thought.

St. Augustine had commanded the newly baptized to love the creed, to study it faithfully, to learn it, and to be able to recite it from memory. They had it from no human source: the articles of faith which appear in the creed are found "scattered through the divine Scriptures."[2] It is the task of the teaching Church to collect the revealed

---

[1] Lanfranc, *De corpore et sanguine Domini*, PL 150: 426 A.

R. L. Poole, *Illustrations of the History of Medieval Thought and Learning*, 2nd. ed., Revised, London, 1920, views the pre-scholastic controversy simply as a phase in the perennial struggle between the authoritarian Church and freedom of thought. In this opinion he is followed to some extent by A. J. Macdonald, *Authority and Reason in the Early Middle Ages*, London, (Oxford University Press), 1933. Neither seems to have particular care for the truth involved in the controversies, but each praises the free-thinkers for their independence regardless of what they taught, even though their ideas would have been extremely harmful to revealed Christianity if they had been permitted to survive. Macdonald rightly blames the collapse of Eastern theology on the close alliance which existed between state and Church in the Eastern Empire; but he assigns all credit for western development to writers outside the central stream: it was the heretics who seized the banner of freedom and the spear of reason.

To answer Macdonald, it may be agreed that heresies provide an occasion for the development of dogma by compelling the best minds in the Church to focus explicit attention upon doctrines which previously had been viewed only in the oblique. But that heresies are a positive cause of development; that error and truth must enter into a necessary and inevitable conflict from which more truth is the necessary outcome: these are relativistic claims which lead inevitably to a denial that any final truth can ever be achieved in religious inquiry. — However, it should be added that in all his writings on pre-scholastic theology, Macdonald is far more temperate than Poole.

[2] St. Augustine, *De symbolo, sermo ad catechumenos*, 1, 1, PL 40: 627: "Ista verba quae audistis, per divinas Scripturas sparsa sunt."

doctrine and reduce it to unity, so that men may more easily retain what they believe, and make profession of their faith.[3] Moreover, the Church must determine the canon of Scripture, both of the Old Testament and of the New.[4] It is under the eye of the Church also that must take place that consistent process of development by which the creed is explained and fortified, against the heretics who have used the very brevity of the creed as a basis for ambiguities.[5] And in any doubt as to the exact meaning of Scripture, the "rule of faith" is to be consulted, which is found in clearer passages of Scripture, and in the authority of the Church.[6]

The great doctor of the west also discussed the relation of faith to natural knowledge, and emphasized the primacy of faith in the famous passage which was to provide the leading principle for St. Anselm's theology, that we believe in order to understand, we do not understand in order to believe.[7] However, though faith is superior to knowledge acquired through natural reason alone, reason has its legitimate part to play in the knowledge of divine things. In reply to the request of Consentius for an explanation of the doctrine of the Trinity, he points out that the request itself is evidence of Consentius' view that the reasoning process must somehow enter into the discussion of the mystery. And Augustine himself is in agreement with this since it is evident that God does not despise that faculty in us which elevates us above lower creatures. When we believe, we do not reject reason, since we would be

---

3 *Ibid.*: "sed inde [i.e. ex Scripturis divinis] collecta et ad unum redacta ne tardorum hominum memoria laboraret; ut omnis homo possit dicere, possit tenere quod credit."

4 *De scriptura sacra Speculum, Praefatio,* CSEL 12: 3: "Quis ignorat in Scripturis sanctis, id est, Legitimis, Propheticis, Evangelicis, et Apostolicis, auctoritate canonica praeditis, quaedam sic esse posita, ut tantum scirentur et crederentur?"

5 *De fide et symbolo,* 1, CSEL 41: 4: "Sed tractatio fidei ad muniendam Symbolum valet: non ut ipsa pro symbolo gratiam Dei consequentibus memoriae mandanda et reddenda tradatur; sed ut illa quae in Symbolo retinentur, contra haereticorum insidias auctoritate catholica et munitore defensione custodiat."

6 *De doctrina Christiana,* 3, 2, PL 34: 65: "Sed cum verba propria faciunt ambiguam Scripturam, primo videndum est ne male distinxerimus aut pronuntiaverimus. Cum ergo adhibita intentio incertum esse perviderit quomodo distinguendum aut quomodo pronuntiandum sit, consulat regulam fidei quam de Scripturarum planioribus locis et Ecclesiae auctoritate percepit."

7 *In St. Joannis Evangelium,* 40, 8, PL 35: 1690: "Quid promittit credentibus, fratres? Et cognoscetis veritatem. Quid enim?—non illam cognoverant, quomodo crediderunt? Non quia cognoverunt crediderunt, sed ut cognoscerent, crediderunt. Credimus enim ut cognoscamus, non cognoscimus ut credamus."

unable even to believe unless we had reasoning minds.[8] Faith in the mysteries must precede our reasoning about them, but even here in a sense reason precedes faith, since it is our reason which urges us to believe.[9]

The pre-scholastic writers followed St. Augustine in acknowledging the primary authority of Scripture and tradition and of the Church. They do not generally treat of these matters systematically, in reflexive studies of the nature of sacred science as such, but their theory of knowledge appears most often in the course of separate polemics, in which the opposing parties are reproached for their failure to follow authority. Against the Adoptianists Alcuin cites St. Paul, Proclus, St. Cyril, St. Hilary, and St. Jerome on the consubstantiality of the Father and the Son, and asks how anyone could be called Catholic who would reject such evangelical and traditional authority.[10] There is, however, no rejection of the *principle* of authority on the part of the adversaries of the truth; rather Alcuin blames their misunderstanding of the Fathers, whose meaning they twist to serve their own ends.[11] The same reproaches will be levelled against Berengar.

Moreover, the pre-scholastic writers upheld not only patristic authority but also the authority of the Church. Prudentius of Troyes cites the Fathers and synodal acts against the enemies of the truth.[12] And he signalizes the special authority of Roman synods.[13] Jonas of Orleans

---

8 *Ep. 120 ad Consentium,* CSEL 34: 706: "Absit namque ut hoc in nobis Deus oderit, in quo nos reliquis animantibus excellentiores creavit. Absit inquam ut ideo credamus, ne rationem accipiamus sive quaeramus; cum etiam credere non possemus, nisi rationales animas haberemus."

9 *Ibid.:* "Ut ergo in quibusdam rebus ad doctrinam salutarem pertinentibus, quas ratione percipere nondum valemus, . . . fides praecedat rationem, . . . et hoc utique rationis est. Proinde ut fides praecedat rationem, rationabiliter iussum est . . . .(quia) ratio qua hoc persuadet, etiam ipsa antecedit fidem."

10 Alcuin, *Adversus Felicem,* 4, 8,PL 101: 181 D: "Quomodo catholicus aestimare potest, qui et tantorum doctorum testimoniis non credit, nec divinae per evangelicas paginas consensit veritati?"

11 *Adversus Elipandum,* 2, 5, PL 101: 261 CD: "Igitur non solum sanctae Scripturae inviolabile sacramentum prava interpretatione maculare niteris, verum etiam sanctorum Patrum multis in locis catholicos sensus depravatos, et ad tui erroris trahere suffragium; . . . veluti in duobos sanctorum Patrum sublimiumque doctorum testimoniis, id est, beati Ambrosii et sancti Augustini verbis ostendi potest. Quam impie, et ab eorum intelligentia longissime interpretaris, quod illi catholico stylo in suis litteris nobis exaratum reliquerunt?"

12 Prudentius of Troyes, *De praedestinatione contra J. Scotum,* PL 115: 1013 CD: "Quanta enim contra diversas haereses maiores nostri egerint, testantur multis totius orbis Patribus sancto spiritu aggregata, testantur acta synodica attestantur etiam doctorum probabilium scripta veridica."

13 *Ibid.,* 1013 D.

insists that the *magisterium* of the Church supplies the rule of faith,[14] that he himself argues "reasonably" upon the basis of Scripture and tradition,[15] and that anyone who would subvert such authority is unreasonable, an author of divisions and superstitions, and guilty of giving scandal to the people.[16]

If any pre-scholastic writer can be effectively cited to show there was no dispute during those centuries concerning the principle of authority, it is surely Joannes Scotus Eriugena, or John the Scot. For this remarkable man, the most brilliant of the ninth century scholars, and surely the best educated, knowing Greek as well as Latin, has been a storm center of discussion down the centuries, his views always held in suspicion by the orthodox, and adopted by the heretics as their own. Berengar claimed erroneously to find in him the justification of his own doctrine, as we shall see, and in our own day a Catholic philosopher such as De Wulf calls him the "father of medieval rationalism."[17]

It is undeniable that certain tendencies existed in his thought which could be exaggerated into heresy, but here it is sufficient to point out that John the Scot was not a rationalist in principle, that he did not attempt to explain the mysteries away, and was not an opponent of authority as a source of religious knowledge. After speaking of the ten categories of being, he insists that God is not properly contained in any of them.[18] The divine mysteries are therefore entirely beyond the grasp of our natural power to understand. Faith is the way to knowledge of God.[19] He refuses to accept Plato's definition of the angels, because it

---

14 Jonas of Orleans, *De cultu imaginum*, 1, PL 106; 309 C: Utique, etsi non ut pridem fidei catholicae regulam, ecclesiasticas traditiones quam venenatis telis per eumdem discipulum suum jaculari nisus sit, breviter memorandum est." (The disciple of Felix is Claudius of Turin, against whom this treatise is written.)

15 *Ibid.*, Lib. 2, col. 362 C: "Hactenus stylo prosecutionis nostrae ex auctoritate divina et sanctorum Patrum doctrina . . . ineptis et stolidissimis oppositionibus rationabiliter obviasse sufficiat."

16 *Ibid.*, Lib. 1, col. 314 D: Ille namque qui irrationabiliter subjectarum sibi plebium mentes scandalizare traditionesque ecclesiasticas tam impudenter reprehendere . . . et auctor schismatum ac superstitionum judicandus est."

17 *History of Medieval Philosophy*, vol. 1, p. 324.

18 John the Scot, *De divisione naturae*, 1, 15, PL 122: 463 C: "Clare conspicio, nulla ratione categorias de natura ineffabili proprie posse praedicari. Nam si aliqua categoriarum de Deo proprie praedicaretur, necessarius genus esse Deus sequeretur. Deus autem nec genus, nec species, nec accidens est. Nulla igitur categoria proprie Deum significare potest."

19 *Com. in Evang. sec. Joan.*, PL 122: 305 A: "Non per aliam viam Dominus corda hominum ingreditur, nisi per fidem, quae via est Domini."

cannot be proved valid by the authority of Scripture and tradition,[20] and he will not comment on the salvation or conversion of the devil, because he says nothing certain upon this point is found in tradition.[21]

This great man is not therefore to be too easily adjudged a heretic, nor ought it be said that he places reason above tradition without quali- fication. He disclaims any intention to teach what is contrary to patris- tic authority, nor to admit definitively that there is conflict among the Fathers;[22] however, he is not clear upon the authority of the *magister- ium* of the Church, the proximate rule of faith, in settling apparent con- flicts, and may be said thereby to open the way to possible exaggerations of private interpretation.[23] And his concept of the divine Wisdom as the common source both of reason and authority can lead to an illu- minism which heretical teachers may adopt as the sole criterion of truth.[24]

To sum up, then, the pre-scholastic position with regard to the value of traditional teaching as a source of religious knowledge, it may be said that they all held in principle for the infallibility of the tradition of the Fathers, however they might disagree as to what that tradition really was. Moreover, it was generally agreed that the teaching Church, whether it was a question of the great Councils of previous centuries or of provincial Councils — with special authority ascribed to the Roman councils under the presidency of the Popes — had power to determine authoritatively the rule of faith,[25] though some tendency towards a

---

20 *De divisione naturae*, PL 122: 762 C: "Quamvis Plato angelum definiat animae rationale et immortale: sed quod auctoritate S. Scripturae sanctorumque Patrum, probare non possumus, inter certas naturarum speculationes, quoniam temerarium est, accipere non debemus."

21 *Ibid.*, col. 941 B: "De salute autem eius [i.e. diaboli] aut conversione, seu in causam suam reditu propterea nihil definire presumimus, quoniam neque divinae historiae, neque sanctorum Patrum, qui eam exposuere, certam de hoc auctoritatem habemus; atque ideo illam obscuritatem silentio honorificamus, ne forte, quae extra nos sunt, quaerere conantes, plus cadere in errorem, quam ascendere in veritatem nobis contingat."

22 *Ibid.*, col. 8 D: "Qui sensui quamvis sanctum Augustinum refragari videatur non omnino tamen, quoniam sancti Basilii est, a nobis repellitur. Non enim nostrum est, de intellectibus sanctorum Patrum dijudicare, sed eos pie et venerabiliter suscipere."

23 *Ibid.*: ". . . non tamen prohibemur eligere, quod magis videtur divinis eloquiis rationis consideratione convenire."

24 *Ibid.*, col. 511 B: "Nulla itaque auctoritas te terreat ab his, quae certae contem- plationis rationabilis suasio edocet. Vera enim auctoritas rectae rationi non obsistit neque recta ratio verae auctoritati. Ambo siquidem ex uno fonte, divina videlicet sapientia, manare dubium non est."

25 A. J. Macdonald, *Reason and Authority in the Early Middle Ages*, p. 5.

weakening of ecclesiastical authority might be found in the neo-Platonist illuminism of John the Scot. And finally, unanimous agreement on the inspiration and inerrancy of Holy Scripture, however unsystematically those concepts might have been understood. When any writer is accused by others of rejecting this weight of authority, it is not so much a question of rejecting the principle as of a culpable misinterpretation, or a twisting of authority to serve his own ends.

If there was substantial agreement among pre-scholastic scholars on the need for fidelity to traditional teaching, they also agreed in assigning a legitimate place to natural reason in the pursuit of knowledge. But the *role* of reason was not autonomous: secular wisdom was not an end in itself, but a means towards a clearer understanding and presentation of religious data. Consequently, all who treat of early medieval philosophy speak of the function of natural reason as "propaedeutic" to divine science. This propaedeutic function was assigned not only to disciplines which we would today classify as philosophical, but also to studies of profane letters and natural science, as these branches were then understood.[26]

---

26 R. L. Poole, *Illustrations of the History of Medieval Thought and Learning*, pp. 2, 3, 4, 6, 21, etc., has much to say about the rejection of classical learning by the medieval Church. The rise of the western Church was accompanied by a rapid decline in the study of classical letters. Rhetorical schools died out; the clergy monopolized education. The Church was altogether inimical to the philosophical spirit. Philosophy was a danger and a snare. If the Church had absorbed and purified the culture of Rome, it might have elevated and refined the barbarians who overran Europe; as it happened, however, the Church was but a step less barbaric than the Teutonic tribes it faced. Cassiodorus opposed this scorn for classical letters, but St. Gregory the Great's influence made the discrediting of classical culture complete. — If Poole wishes to commend a teacher in the main stream of Catholic tradition, he tries to take him out of the Catholic tradition; for example, in his comments on St. Anselm, p. 91, Poole denies that St. Anselm is a "scholastic," and calls him "the last of the Fathers" instead of the pioneer of developed scholasticism which he is.

The charges of Poole reflect an attitude of mind once almost universal among non-Catholics, but gradually falling into the discard as medieval scholarship becomes more disinterested. — It is true that some Fathers seemed to wish a complete break with pagan learning. They were deeply imbued with the Pauline idea that Christianity was not a philosophy but a life, that the wisdom of the Cross was foolishness to the pagan philosopher. Paganism was the adversary in the field; it had its philosophy, and consequently that philosophy must be attacked. But at the same time Christianity was extremely rich in its ideas, and drew converts who were themselves philosophers, Clement and Origen, and the Latin apologists for example. We see in the development of Christian wisdom a rather paradoxical attack on classical culture carried on by Christians who were themselves first-rate classicists. This inconsistency is only apparent, and was inevitable in an incipient Christian culture. It has often been pointed out that Tertullian denouncing rhetoric is himself a superb rhetorician, and that St. Gregory making little of the importance of the grammar of the Bible uses perfect grammar himself. — The reader is referred to treatments of this topic in E. Gilson, *Reason and Revelation in the Middle*

As in the realm of authority, so in that of the value of human reason, St. Augustine formed medieval thought. If pagan philosophy has in it anything of truth, this is not to be feared, but to be taken over by the Christians as rightful possessors,[27] just as the Israelites at the divine command took over the spoils of the Egyptians.[28] Not all of the teachings of the Gentiles are to be shunned as superstitions: the liberal disciplines may be put to the service of the truth, and even the ethical teachings of the philosophers contain much that is true regarding the worship of God.[29] And St. Augustine says rightly that the advice which he gives them is not new or revolutionary, but merely a recommendation that they continue the practice long since adopted by the greatest Christian writers, both Greek and Latin.[30]

In the *De ordine,* St. Augustine not only commends the usefulness of profane science, but holds it an essential possession in one who would be worthy of the title of learned.[31] Here he is not speaking of rational knowledge in a general way, as equated with common sense, but as a technical science to be learned from the seven liberal disciplines.

---

27 *De doctrina Christiana,* 2, 40, 60-61, PL 34: 63: "Philosophi autem qui vocantur, si qua forte vera et fidei nostrae accomodata dixerunt, maxime Platonici, non solum formidanda non sunt, sed ab eis tamquam injustis possessoribus in usum nostrum vindicanda."

28 This comparison, dating from patristic times (Cf. St. Jerome, Ep. 70, ad Magnum oratorem urbis Romanae, PL 22: 667, and St. Augustine, *loc cit.*), served throughout the Middle Ages as the Scriptural justification for the propaedeutic *role* of the seven liberal arts. It is found in Cassiodorus, *De inst. div. lit.,* 28, PL 70: 1142; Alcuin, *Ep.* 307, MGH (Epistolae) 4: 470; Walafrid Strabo, *Glossa ordinaria,* PL 113: 193, 220-221, 474; Prudentius of Troyes, *De praed. contra J. Scotum,* PL 115: 1016; Raban Maur, *De cler. inst.,* 3, 26, PL 107: 404; Rathier of Verona, *Ep. 3,* PL 136: 650; St. Peter Damian, Serm. 6 de S. Eleuchadio, PL 144: 540-541. For other citations, see De Ghellinck, *Le mouvement théologique* . . . , Chap. 1, Appendix B, pp. 67-70.

29 *De doctrina Christiana,* 2, 40, PL 34: 63: "sed etiam liberales disciplinas usui veritates aptiores, et quaedam praecepta utilissima continent deque ipso uno Deo colendo nonnulla vera inveniuntur apud eos."

30 *Ibid.;* "Nam quid aliud fecerunt multi boni fideles nostri? Nonne adspicimus quanto auro argento et veste suffarcinatus exierit de Aegypto Cyprianus doctor suavissimus et martyr beatissimus? quanto Lactantius? quanto Victorinus, Optatus, Hilarius, ut de vivis taceam? quanto innumerabiles Graeci?"

31 *De ordine,* 2, 16, CSEL 63: 177: "Eruditi dignissimus nomine non temere iam quaerit illa divina, non iam credenda solum, sed etiam contemplanda, intelligenda, atque retinenda."

Ages, New York, 1938, and E. K. Rand, *Founders of the Middle Ages,* Chapters 1 and 2 (see especially p. 64).

The charge of Poole that the Church failed to adopt the civilization of Rome in order to civilize the barbarians is a curious inversion of the much more common assertion that the Church simply took over the imperial structure bodily and made of the *imperium* a papal theocracy. For a brilliant apologetical analysis of this practice of levelling contrary charges against the Church, see G. K. Chesterton, *Orthodoxy,* New York, 1941, Chapter 6, "The Paradoxes of Christianity."

He speaks in the *De ordine* of the propaedeutic *role* of reason only after he has defined and distinguished the seven liberal arts. And for the propaedeutic function, the art of dialectics holds the highest place. It is the art of definition, of analysis, of synthesis; its function to make an orderly arrangement of knowledge; it protects the truth against the assaults of error; it teaches one to teach and another to learn. It is the discipline of disciplines, the instrument of knowledge.[32] The systematized knowledge which it gives is indispensable to one who would pursue safely the knowledge of God and of man.[33]   Dialectic is of value in every inquiry into sacred science,[34] but it must be applied with care, so as to avoid willful quibbling and childish ostentation.[35] For the use of the liberal arts is most difficult, and demands constant application and unremitting study from one's earliest days.[36]

For the pre-scholastic theologians, the principal value of the liberal arts consisted in the refutation of heresies.[37] And the most brilliant among all of the ninth-century scholars assigned a threefold function to the dialectical art: to make doubtful things clear, to serve in ancillary *role* the progress of rational investigation, and to give orderly arrangement to acquired knowledge.[38] But John the Scot follows St. Augus-

---

32 *Ibid.*, 2, 13, CSEL 63: 174: "Nam eam definiendo distribuendo colligendo non solum digesserat atque ordinarat, verum ab omni etiam falsitatis ireptione defenderat. Quando ergo transiret ad alia fabricanda, nisi ipsa sua prius quasi quaedam machinamenta et instrumenta distingueret, notaret, digereret, proderetque ipsam disciplinam disciplinarum, quam dialecticam vocant? Haec docet docere, haec docet discere."

33 *Ibid.*, 2, 16, p. 177: "Quisquis autem vel adhuc servus cupiditatum et inhians rebus pereuntibus; vel iam ista fugiens casteque vivens nesciens tamen, quid sit nihil, quid informis materia, quid formatum exanime, quid corpus, quid exanime in corpore . . . quisquis ista nesciens, non dico de summo illo Deo, qui scitur melius nesciendo, sed de anima ipsa sua quarere ac disputare voluerit, tantum errabit quantum errari plurimum potest."

34 *De doctrina Christiana*, 2, 31, 48, PL 34: 57-58: "sed disputationis disciplina ad omnia genera quaestionum, quae in litteris sanctis sunt penetranda et dissolvenda."

35 *Ibid.*: "tantum ibi cavenda est libido rixandi, et puerilis quaedam ostentatio decipiendi adversarium."

36 *De ordine*, 2, 16, CSEL 63: 178: "usum earum assequi difficillimum est nisi ei qui ab ipsa pueritia ingeniosissimus instantissime atque constantissime operam dederit."

37 Alcuin, *De grammatica*, PL 101: 853D: "Sunt igitur gradus, quos quaeritis, et . . . grammatica, rhetorica, dialectica, arithmetica, geometria, musica, et astrologia. . . . Iis quoque sancti et catholici nostrae fidei doctores et defensores omnibus haeresiarchis in contentionibus publicis semper superiores exstiterunt."
Cf. Raban Maur, *De inst. cler.*, 3, 20, PL 107: 379 C D.

38 John the Scot, *De div. naturae*, PL 122: 474 D: "Non tam late patent dialectici loci, ut undecumque dialecticus animus in natura rerum argumentum, quod rei dubiae facit fidem, repererit, locum argumenti esse desribat, seu argumenti sedem."
Ibid., 475 A: Dialectica est communium animi conceptionum rationabilium diligens investigatrixque disciplina."
Ibid., 486 B: "Dialecticae . . . proprietas est, rerum omnium, quae intelligi possunt, naturas dividere, coniungere, discernere, propriusque locos unicuique distribuere."

tine in warning against an improper use of dialectics. Both the moral virtues and the arts, he says, are alike in having their origin from God, but they differ in that virtues cannot be ill used, while dialectics can be used for good or for evil, for good in the discernment of truth, for evil in the confusion of the simple through false arguments.[39]

This, then, is the principle of harmony upon which there was substantial agreement among the pre-scholastic scholars: authority — whether Scriptural, patristic, or conciliar — must be followed, and reason has its legitimate propaedeutic and polemic functions in the pursuit of religious knowledge. Yet it is a fact that in the application of that principle there was no agreement at all. The intellectual life of the three pre-scholastic centuries issued in bitter theological disputations and irreconcilable opposition.[40]

2. *Controversy in the Application of the Principle*

The controversies of the pre-scholastic period cannot be explained by any difference of background or education among the men who took part in them. They were the same men who were building the school culture. They all had the same background: St. Augustine and the Latin tradition of the Fathers, and the gradual tradition of Aristotelian logic—a community of inspiration which cannot explain theological conflicts. Two causes seem best to explain the diversity of thought

---

39 *Ibid.*, 382 BC: "Potest enim aliquis in disciplina, verbi causa, disputandi, quae dicitur dialectica, peritus, quae nullo dubitante a Deo homini donatur, si voluerit, bene uti, quoniam ad hoc certissime data est dum ea ignorantes eam erudit, vera falsaque discernit confusa dividit, separata collingit, in omnibus veritatem inquirit. Potest e contrario perniciose vivere (uti) ad quod non est data, dum falsa pro veris approbans, alios in errorem mittat. . . ."

Further testimonies to the values of dialectics, in addition to those cited *supra*, n. 28, are the following: St. Isidore, *Etymologiae*, 1, 2, and 22-23, etc., PL 82: 74, 128 C, 140-154; Pope Eugene II, *Decr.*, MGH (Leges) 2: app. p. 100; Heriger of Lobbes, *De corp. et sang. Dom.*, 7, PL 139: 185 B. The attitude of Lanfranc and Berengar will be brought out in Chapter 3 of this study.

40 G. Brunhes, *La foi chrétienne et la philosophie, au temps de la Renaissance carolingienne*, pp. 25-26: "The personal exercise of intellectual activity in the ninth century is carried on almost exclusively in connection with theological controversies. If we except a few pages of Fredegise and the *De divisione naturae* of John the Scot, where, moreover, philosophy and theology are continually intermingled, we can say that all the writings of this period, over and above mere school-books, are works of polemic and religious controversy." The history of thought in the ninth century, and in the eleventh as well, is necessarily the history of the theological controversies which fill it. The substance of these controversies does not concern us here, except in so far as the methods used have bearing on the formation of scholasticism. The great theological questions were those of Images (Jonas of Orleans vs. Agobard of Lyons and Claudius of Turin; of the "Filioque" (Theodulph of Orleans); of Adoptianism (Alcuin vs. Felix and Elipand); of Predestination (Hincmar and Raban Maur vs. Gottschalk); and of the Eucharist (Paschasius vs. Ratramn).

among these scholars: first, the fact that throughout the period there was almost completely absent a definite distinction between the domains of philosophy and of Christian faith; and second, a characteristic of the incipient dialectic itself, which led certain "speculative" writers to exaggerate the *role* of reason, and aroused immediate reaction on the part of more "practical" and conservative scholars.

The question of the relation of reason and authority was complicated first by the almost general failure of pre-scholastic theologians to distinguish clearly between the two orders of knowledge. In the ninth century, "religion and philosophy are not . . . two disciplines entirely distinct and heterogeneous as we consider them today. To understand the minds of these authors, we must put aside our habitual mode of thinking. . . . For Alcuin, for Raban Maur, for all their pupils, the basic thought, the point of departure of all their reflections is the community of object, of method, of conditions of research, between philosophy and religious knowledge, or what may be called 'theology'."[41] In the education which they received, philosophical data are confused pell-mell with the data of faith, and the same confusion is apparent in their literature: it is not at all uncommon for a ninth-century writer to include in what he considers to be a closely reasoned argument based on natural reason alone a premise which contains a mystery knowable only by faith. Thus it is that some writers, without knowing it, tend to suppress the proper object of faith by absorbing it into demonstrations of reason, while others deny reason its legitimate authority in favor of an absolute dependence on faith.

It is evident that for Alcuin and Raban Maur no clear distinction existed between philosophy and religious knowledge. It is true that Alcuin's definition of philosophy is acceptable even from the modern viewpoint of separate philosophy, since its religious implications might well apply to the branch called natural theology:

> Philosophia est naturarum inquisitio, rerum humanarum divinarumque cognitio, quantum homini possibile est aestimare.[42]

But immediately he takes philosophy out of the realm of pure speculation by attaching to philosophy moral implications, and giving it a religious definition:

> Est quoque philosophia honestas vitae, studium bene vivendi, medi-

---

41 G. Brunhes, *op. cit.*, p. 53.

42 Alcuin, *De dialectica,* PL 101: 952 A. Cf. almost identical definition in Raban Maur, *De universo,* 15, 1, PL 111: 416.

tatio mortis, contemptus saeculi, quod magis convenit Christianis, qui saeculi ambitione calcata, disciplinabili similitudine futurae patriae vivunt.[43]

And it is not merely in the moral order that Alcuin identifies philosophy and religious knowledge. More radically yet, when he divides philosophy into three parts, he places the sacred books within one or other of the classifications.[44] The result of his definition and division is that for him philosophy is nothing else but universal science, that it comprehends the whole ensemble of human knowledge. His definition of philosophy includes *all* the branches of the liberal arts, including disciplines now considered scientific rather than philosophical.[45]

With such a concept of philosophy as universal science, lacking any distinction from religious knowledge, it is not surprising to see Alcuin make a free use of dialectical arguments in matters of faith. Speaking of the category of relation, he argues that the co-eternity of the Son with the Father is a conclusion of dialectical necessity.[46]

---

43 *Ibid.* This moral definition is reproduced by Raban Maur, PL 111: 416. Further indication that Raban Maur did not distinguish religious from philosophical knowledge is found in the fact that he taught the necessity of divine grace to arrive at any truth: *De videndo Deum*, 1, PL 112: 1280.

44 *Ibid.* "Carolus: 'In quot partes dividitur philosophia? Alc.: 'In tres: physicam, ethicam, et logicam . . . in his quippe generibus philosophiae etiam eloquia divina consistunt. . . . Nam aut de natura disputare solent ut in Genesi et in Ecclesiaste; aut de moribus, ut in Proverbiis et in omnibus sparsim libribus; aut de logica pro qua nostri theologicam sibi vindicant ut in Canticis canticorum et sancto Evangelio.'"

45 Schematically, Alcuin divides philosophy as follows (*Ibid.*):

philosophy	physical	arithmetic geometry music astronomy
	ethical	prudence justice temperance fortitude
	logical	dialectic rhetoric

46 *De dialectica*, 5, PL 101; 959: "Et sciendum est quod semper relativa vel simul nasci vel simul exstingui oportet, ut subtracto servo dominus non est; remoto domino nec servus apparet. Ita de patre et filio. Ac ideo secundum hanc categoriae regulam miranda est Arii, vel magis miseranda, et eius quoque sociorum stulta caecitas; asserentes Filium secundum tempus Patri esse posteriorem; dum omnino constat secundum dialecticam simul consempiternum esse Filium cum Patre. Et si Deus Pater (quod nec illorum impietas suadebat negare) aeternus est, utique et Filius aeternus est secundum dialecticae rationis necessitatem." — For other examples of Alcuin's free use of dialectical arguments in matters of faith without any attempt to distinguish between the two sources of knowledge, see PL 100: 431-436 (Redemption) and MGH (Epist. Karol. Aevi) 2: 337 ff. (Adoptianism, the divine sonship, and the virginal birth.)

Alcuin's failure to distinguish between philosophical and religious knowledge is apparent in his discussions with his pupil Fredegise.[47] Fredegise brought to the question of the Trinity an entirely rational approach from which all mystery was excluded. It is not so significant that Alcuin should have made some response to Fredegise, but it is significant that he should have answered his objections one by one, without stating as a principle to answer them all the distinction between the realm of philosophy and that of faith. Alcuin himself seems wholly unconscious of the danger that lurked in the confusion of the two domains. Neither Alcuin nor Agobard of Lyons accuses Fredegise of unorthodoxy. Fredegise is not an "adversary" of the faith; Alcuin and Agobard are not "opponents" of dialectics. Granted that the questions raised by Fredegise were puerile, taken in themselves, yet they hinted at great problems. Fredegise had been taught dialectics, and he wanted to apply it to the hilt. He had learned his philosophy and theology pellmell: no one had distinguished for him their respective fields.

It has been pointed out that John the Scot was not an adversary of the principle of authority, especially that of Scripture and the Fathers, and that he spoke of dialectics as occupying an ancillary place. But more categorically than anyone else he identified philosophy and religious knowledge,[49] and in some passages he seems to give precedence to reason over authority as ultimate source of religious knowledge.[50] It is an oversimplification to set down such passages as evi-

---

47 Fredegise is the author of one of the few works of separate philosophy of the Carolingian age, *De nihilo et tenebris*, PL 105: 751-756 a work of pure speculation, meant to prove the real existence of *nothing* and *darkness*. Fredegise is the outstanding Carolingian example of the "speculative" rationalizing tendency. His writing has no moral or educative purpose; he brings to properly religious questions a pretentious dialectical approach which is backed up with rudimentary dialectical skill. His practice was to adopt an absurdly literal interpretation of Scripture, and then to argue to his conclusion through a puerile process of logic-chopping. For example, he argues (753 C) that darkness must exist because it says in Genesis that darkness was upon the face of the deep; (754 C) because David says that the Lord sends darkness ("Si non sunt," asks Fredegise, "quomodo mittuntur?"); and (754D) because Christ says that the wicked shall be cast out into the exterior darkness "Extra enim, unde exterius derivatus est, locum significat.")

48 *Ep. ad Fredegisum*, PL 101: 57-64.

49 John the Scot, *De praed.*, 1, 5, 1, PL 122: 357-358: "Quid est aliud de philosophia tractare, nisi verae religionis, qua summa et principalis omnium rerum causa, Deus, et humiliter colitur, et rationabiliter investigatur regulas exponere? Conficitur inde, veram esse philosophiam veram religionem, convertimque veram religionem esse veram philosophiam."

50 *De divisione naturae*, 1, 69, PL 122: 513 B: "Rationem priorem esse natura . . . didicimus . . . auctoritate siquidem ex vera ratione processit, ratio vero nunquam ex auctoritate. Omnes enim auctoritas quae vera ratione non approbatur infirma videtur esse. Vera autem ratio, quoniam suis virtutibus data atque immutabilis munitur, nullius auctoritas astipulatione roborari indiget."

dence that John the Scot is a rationalist and an adversary of Scripture and tradition; yet there appear in his theory of knowledge an individualism and illuminism which are not in the Catholic tradition.[51] John the Scot cannot be called unorthodox or heretical, but he did continue the confusion between the two realms: for him, faith and reason have not two objects formally distinct, and no clear distinction exists between the natural and supernatural order. Brunhes finds in this confusion the explanation of John the Scot's enthusiastic reception by the heretics and the suspicion with which he has always been viewed by the orthodox. "He condemns himself to be misunderstood in his good intentions by the orthodox, and to become naturally the patron of those who in centuries to come, put themselves in opposition to the general current of theological thought."[52] And in fact, notwithstanding his superior brilliance and education, his contemporaries were to have a greater influence on the formation of western theological thought. He was too closely attached to the past, while they were in touch with new problems. Giving themselves at first too naively to dialectics to explain the mysteries of faith, they felt its dangers by experience of the individualism of John and the heresies of others, and they set about establishing a harmony between the two fields of knowledge.

The second factor that led to theological controversy during the pre-scholastic period was the tendency of certain writers to adopt an exaggerated position either in favor of dialectics or against it. It must be remembered that rational speculation, avowedly legitimate in principle, did not appear in the pre-scholastic period as mere common sense, or even as a system of thought Christian in origin, but as a technical discipline from the pagan past. The thought of Aristotle and Plato formed the framework of philosophical speculation, with Aristotle bearing the predominant part. Mandonnet has pointed out that one of the striking characteristics of medieval intellectual life is the diversity of attitude in the presence of ideas and systems handed down from classical antiquity.[53] Notwithstanding its excellence, the work of Aristotle possessed within it certain characteristics, which would arouse violent opposition. It was established on a basis of abstract and experimental science: hence it would be offensive to mystics. It was conceived apart

---

51 For statements of the priority of reason over authority, see *De divisione naturae*, cols. 513 BC, 511 B, 781 CD. Cf. Macdonald, *Reason and Authority in the Early Middle Ages*, p. 47, and Brunhes, *op. cit.*, p. 173.

52 Brunhes, *op. cit.*, p. 173.

53 Mandonnet, *Siger de Brabant et l'averroisme latin au XIIIe siècle*, p. 19.

from any religious system: hence it would leave outside of consideration some of the philosophical truths which the great monotheistic religions placed at the foundation of their beliefs. Wherever Aristotle
appeared, the same reactions took place with astonishing regularity.[54]
At the beginning, Aristotle by the power of his thought makes his en-
trance and captivates minds. As the work proceeds, it evokes from
religious souls opposition sometimes to the point of declared war; while
on the other hand minds drawn to independent speculation, or inclined
to use it even across the boundaries of religious teaching, accept it whole
and entire as the symbol of liberty of thought, and seek to apply its ir-
resistible laws to faith. Finally, between the two extremes, the most
clear-sighted thinkers, convinced of the value of Aristotle, were at the
same time bold enough to judge him and respectful enough to religion
not to transgress it—and thus brought the two into accord.

Along the same line of thought, the theory of Brunhes is admirably
complementary to that of Mandonnet. Brunhes explains the double
tendency of the period not only in the temperament of the men involved, but also in the various positions which they held in the Church and
the various responsibilities which bound them. Some men, Agobard,
Hincmar, Prudentius, for example, were bishops, without leisure for
disinterested speculation. They were interested in forming Christians,
and their philosophy was geared to the practical. Hence, in them philosophy will have a moral application, and their scholarly work will consist in the mere copying or abridgement of past works, without much
creative thought. And they will take exception to novelties of speculation which might disturb the beliefs of the faithful.

On the other hand, there were men not involved in social responsibilities, the monk, Gottschalk, for example, and the scholar, John the
Scot. These men might cultivate reason more boldly, and develop dialectics more independently. This dialectical movement in its earliest
stages was mainly a movement of monks: they alone had sufficient leisure, once the work of clearing and civilizing was well on its way to accomplishment. Necessarily their interest led to dialectics: it appealed
to their combative barbarian instincts, it gave itself to methodical handling; and finally, it was *available,* the only systematized discipline with
which the independent mind could exercise itself upon the body of acquired truth, which was entirely religious.[55]

---

54 *Ibid.*, p. 23.
55 G. Brunhes, *op. cit.*, pp. 71-83.

Thus we see that despite an agreement in principle and theory on the legitimacy of rational speculation in religious matters, the intellectual temper of the age tended towards a divergence in application and practice, and towards the formation of opposed schools, the "practicals" and the "speculatives." The former were conservative, adhering to tradition and authority, the later radical, eager to try their skill at the entrancing game of logic, even though the most sacred of beliefs provided the object for their speculation.

The struggle against the rationalizing tendencies of ninth-century dialecticians was carried on in the provincial Councils and in the writing of individual scholars. Against the Adoptianist heresy, which persisted in emphasizing the humanity of Christ to the detriment of the divine nature, the Council of Frankfort rightly insisted that both natures enter into the mystery of the Incarnation.[56] The great scholar, Servatus Lupus, abbot of Ferriéres, writes to Charles the Bald that Catholic faith in the doctrine of predestination is founded on Scripture and tradition; as do Prudentius of Troyes, and Florus of Lyons.[57] One result of the "practical" tendency was to remove from the competence of pure reason the data of certain mysteries. This was the result achieved at the Councils, and if the "practicals" did not succeed in breaking down all opposition, they were able at least to reduce the heretics to silence. Felix and Gottschalk must renounce their ideas, or at least keep silence. The importance of the silence imposed on the heretics was to impose a limit to the domain of reason and to draw a line of demarcation. As source of religious knowledge, reason and tradition began to be regarded as distinct, though the relations of the two were not any too clearly worked out.[58]

---

56 *Conc. Francofordiensis Epistola synodica ad praesules Hispaniae missa, refutatoria prioris epistolae eorumdem,* PL 101: 1331 B: "Sanctus Augustinus dicit in sermone de nativitate Christi: merito, dilectissimi, miranda est salvatoris nostri Nativitas, non solum illa divina, de qua dictum est: In principio erat Verbum; sed etiam illa humana, de qua idem dicit Evangelista: Verbum caro factum est. Unde et propheta, generationem quis enarrabit? Divina enim magis fide veneranda sunt quam ratione investiganda."

57 Servatus Lupus, *Ep. 128,* PL 119: 605 B: Hanc fidem [de praedestinatione] tenuerunt Ecclesiae catholicae invictissimi defensores. Hanc ego minimus omnium custodio . . . nec . . . inaniter, hoc est, vanae gloriae studio cupio innotescere, . . . sed asserendae veritatis intuitu quod in divinis auctoritatibus eorumque sensum sequentibus praecellentissimis auctoribus Deo inspirante deprehendi quaerentibus absque contentione manifesto."
Cf. Prudentius, *De praed. contra J. Scotum,* PL 115: 1013-1014; 1021; and Florus, *Adv. J. Scotum Erig.,* PL 119: 101.

58 Brunhes, *op. cit.,* pp. 65-69; 125.

Florus, the deacon of Lyons, was one of those who in the ninth century adopted the moderate position and at the same time contributed greatly to the knowledge of the real distinction between the formal object of faith and that of natural reason. He disputed against the oversimplified theology of Hincmar and against the excessive subtlety of John the Scot as well. He did not deny all utility to dialectics, but insisted that it may be used only for a deeper understanding of the truths already believed on the motive of faith.[59]

In the tenth century, the question of religious knowledge began in general to revolve more closely about that doctrine where it was to receive its greatest test, the doctrine of the Eucharist. Rathier of Verona took an anti-dialectical position, arguing that the Eucharist is a mystery to be received by faith, and not to be reasoned about;[60] but Heriger of Lobbes not only proclaimed the utility of this discipline even in questions bearing on the Mystery of Faith, but also assigned to dialectics divine origin, since it emanates from a law of nature laid down by the Author of all the arts.[61] And in his treatise on the Eucharist, written to conciliate Paschasius and Ratramn, Heriger made stout use of dialectics.[62]

At the beginning of the eleventh century, Fulbert, the great master at Chartres, expressed a wise and moderate viewpoint which proves that the extreme rationalism of Berengar of Tours cannot be explained from the teaching which he received from Fulbert. In his letter to Adeo-

---

59 Florus, *Adv. J. Scot. Erig.*, PL 119: 230 D - 231 A: "Quod non ideo dicimus quasi nihil in illis etiam litteris humanis inveniatur veritas, aut illae disciplinae non habeant aliquam utilitatem ad indagandam veritatem; sed quia omni fideli homini primum vigilantissime discenda est veritas fidei ex auctoritate Scripturarum Dei: ut quid postea de eisdem humanis litteris legere, aut sciri necesse fuerit, totum ex illa divina auctoritate et fidei veritate dijudicetur; ut si quid ibi ab eius regula non discedat absque periculo recipiatur, quidquid ab ea dissonare inveniatur quasi mortiferum respuatur. Quisquis autem putat se absque verae fidei cognitione, absque Scripturae sanctae fidelissima auctoritate absque paternae doctrinae studiosissima institutione solis humanis litteris et disciplinis indagare posse veritatem Dei, et fidei integritatem, procul dubio seipsum illudit et decipit; et dum vult videri quasi inventor veritatis, magister erroris efficitur."

60 Rathier of Verona, *Ep. Ia ad Patricium*, PL 136: 648 A: "De ceteris, quaeso ne solliciteris, quandoquidem mysterium esse audis, et hoc fidei; nam si mysterium est, non valet comprehendi: si fidei, debet credi, non vero discuti."

61 Heriger of Lobbes, *De corpore et sanguine Domini* [wrongly attributed to Gerbert] PL 139: 185 B: "Non enim ars illa, quae dividit genera in species et species in genera resolvit, ab humanis machinationibus est facta; sed in natura rerum ab Auctore omnium artium, quae verae artes sunt, et a sapientibus inventa, et ad utilitatem solveris rerum indaginis est usitata."

62 *Ibid.*, 188 D: Sed iam forti syllogismo quod praemisimus, concludamus. Dixeramus Dominum non de spiritualibus escis, sed de carnalibus dixisse, omne quod intrat in os, et reliqua."

datus,[63] Fulbert writes that the divine counsels are incomprehensibly deep, and merely human wisdom cannot fathom them. Many, he says, are attempting to scrutinize these depths, and are falling into the darkness of error. Worldly wisdom, outwardly eloquent, inwardly empty, is always seeking, and never finding, because the depths of the divine mysteries are revealed not to human disputation, but to the eyes of faith. Three things are necessary for spiritual progress, and in them all salvation consists: to understand and to firmly hold the mystery of the Trinity and the oneness of God; to know the nature of Baptism; and to understand the two sacraments of life, in which the Body and Blood of the Lord are contained. Many are examining even these three truths, trusting more to carnal sense than to faith, are falling into error, and are neither perceiving the truth, nor enjoying the virtue of the sacraments. These are masters of error, preferring darkness to light. But along with such exhortations to humility and faith, Fulbert strongly encouraged the development of rational speculation: in the library of Chartres as in no other center was centralized the entire tradition of dialectics which had come down through Boethius and Cassiodorus, and Isidore and Alcuin.

The eleventh century witnessed a tremendous expansion of dialectical argument applied to divine mysteries. The fascination of dialectics was intense, and some minds were so overcome as to subordinate even the Bible to reason, which became the basis of their approach to faith. Among the doctrines which became subject to criticism were those concerning the divinity and the virginal birth of Christ.[64] We do not have much direct knowledge of the teachings of these "dialectici moderni," but find repeated references to them in the writings of their orthodox adversaries, principally St. Peter Damian, Manegold of Lautenbach, and Othloh of Ratisbon.[65] St. Peter Damian is the eleventh century writer who most staunchly opposed the excesses of the dialecticians. But St. Peter Damian must not be set down unreservedly as an adversary of secular learning. True, he gave it a secondary place, but he sought

---

63 PL 141: 196-197. The authenticity of this letter is verified in Clerval, *Les Écoles de Chartres*, p. 42. It is cited by Durand of Troarn in PL 149: 1405, and attributed by Durand to Fulbert.

64 See De Ghellinck, "Réminiscences de la dialectique de Marius Victorinus dans les conflits théologiques du XIe et du XIIe siècles," *Revue neo-scholastique*, 18 (1911) 432-435.

65 See, for example, St. Peter Damian, PL 145: 603 CD, 611 B; PL 144: 362 A; Manegold of Lautenbach, PL 155: 163 A; Othloh of Ratisbon, PL 146: 60-62.

it for himself and encouraged it for others; and he sent his nephew to Gaul to gain it.[66]

As a final comment on the theory of religious knowledge in pre-scholastic times, it may be said that the men did not realize they were creating problems by their confusion between philosophy and faith. They lacked the experience to make classifications, and they did not possess the instruments of work. It was only the danger of heresy born of this confusion that caused them to feel the gravity and the importance of the problems. It must be granted that the arguments of the "dialectici" in the eleventh century amounted more to an intellectual gymnastic sought for its own sake than to a serious development of theological method. But if a master should appear who would push the rational principle to the limit of a virtual rejection of traditional teaching; and if he should in turn be opposed by men who were as well versed in dialectics as himself, but who accepted the teaching of the Catholic Church as the proximate rule of faith—from such a conflict we might rightfully expect to see a clarification of method and a substantial advance in theology. The eleventh century provided such a conflict in the Berengarian controversy, and out of it resulted a long step towards the flowering of scholasticiasm, and a rich development of Eucharistic theology.

---

66 J. P. Whitney, *Hildebrandine Essays*, Cambridge, Engl., 1932, Ch. 5, "Berengar of Tours, pp. 158-179. Cf. St. Peter Damian, *Opusc.* 14, PL 145: 334 and *Opusc. 15*, PL 145: 350.

CHAPTER III

The Theological Principles of Berengar and of His Catholic Opponents

It is established that the pre-scholastic theologians agreed in assigning a lawful function to rational speculation in the search for religious truth. Authority was of paramount importance, of course: the authority of God revealing, through Scripture and authentic tradition; and more proximately, the authority of the teaching Church, official interpreter of the divine word. But the traditional authorities needed to be organized, systematized, clarified: the divine message was scattered through the Scriptures, the creeds were short; upon some points the Church had not spoken. For this work of analysis and synthesis, the scholars had at their disposal an imperfect philosophical instrument, the dialectics of the schools. Their theory of religious knowledge may be expressed hierarchically: first, the inviolability of authority; second, the utility of reason, in an auxiliary and dependent role. If any writer seemed to invert the order, it was not because he had it in mind to contradict the divine tradition in the name of reason, but because in the inevitable confusion which attended upon the birth of a new science he failed to distinguish adequately between the competencies of the two orders of knowledge.

Consequently, if it happens that in the middle of the eleventh century Berengar of Tours will make a strong appeal to reason, he cannot upon this ground alone be called a pioneer. In applying the science of logic to theology he was merely continuing an established principle. But in *building* his theology on logic, in placing dialectics as the foundation and first principle of his theology, he inverted the order beyond all question, and thus separated himself from the pre-scholastic stream. That is the basic position of this study: that the error of Berengar of Tours lay at a deeper level than any aspect of Eucharistic theology which was involved. He was a heretic on principle before he touched the Eucharist. In rejecting the traditional teaching and approaching the Mystery of Faith from the viewpoint of an immature philosophy, he fell into a philosophical error which was in turn the deep reason for his theological error. The purpose of this study is to establish this position.

33

It is incorrect, then, to speak of a positive contribution by Berengar to theology or to the scholastic method. On the contrary, his direct influence was inimical to both: by his excessive reliance on dialectics, he gave strength to the reaction against intellectualism which was going on in the monasteries. One can at most speak of an indirect contribution, since his errors called forth in reply a series of excellent monographs which otherwise might never have been written. These were the work of men themselves skilled in dialectics, able to face the heresiarch on his own ground; but at the same time they were the work of Catholics, who retained the proper balance between legitimate rational inquiry and the authority of tradition: which in theology is reason's stabilizing norm. The great development of theology which resulted from the Berengarian controversy received its impetus, not from the heretic, but from his Catholic opponents. Their phflosophy was no more mature than that of Berengar, but they used it in dependence on faith; and through the harmony which they effected between the two elements, faith and reason, they were able to carry the Eucharistic theology to a point of development which it had not reached before.

It is not necessary for the purposes of this study to set down at length the history of the Berengarian controversy. That has already been written.[1] But a brief survey of the literature is necessary to mark

---

1 A. J. Macdonald, *Berengar and the Reform of Sacramental Doctrine*, London, 1930: an extensive and detailed historical study, it fixes the events of the controversy; but on the historical side it exaggerates the importance of political considerations, and on the doctrinal side it attempts to present the Berengarian doctrine as the genuine medieval tradition, and the Paschasian-Lanfranc doctrine as a gross and contradictory innovation.

R. Heurtevent, *Durand de Troarn et les origines de l'hérésie bérengarienne*, Paris, 1912: an excellent study, includes the ninth century background, but covers only the early stages of the controversy, 1047-1060.

J. Geiselmann, *Die Eucharististielehre der Vorscholastik*, Paderborn, 1926: exhaustive study of entire pre-scholastic Eucharistic theology.

M. Cappuyns, "Bérenger de Tours," *Dictionnaire d'histoire et de géographie ecclésiastique* (DHGE), 8 (1934) 385-407: summarizes authentic history of the controversy, including the findings of Macdonald; has a selected, up-to-date bibliography.

F. Vernet, "Bérenger de Tours," *Dictionnaire de théologie catholique* (DTC), 2 (1905) 722-742; G. Sauvage, C.S.C., "Berengarius of Tours," *The Catholic Encyclopedia*, 2 (1907) 487-489.

Berengar (ca. 1000-1088) studied at Chartres under Fulbert; *Scholasticus* at St. Martin's School at Tours, 1031; Archdeacon of Angers, 1041. His Eucharistic teachings first came under ecclesiastical notice at Council of Rome in 1050. There his doctrine was condemned along with that of John the Scot (Ratramn). Further condemnations at Vercelli (1050), Paris (1051), Rome (1059), Rome (1079), where he signed a formula in which the words *substantialiter converti* appear for the first time in an ecclesiastical document (DB 355). Retired from public life, and died about 1088, at peace with the church. He was of blameless life, angelic purity, extremely charitable to the poor. But the evidence points to a great fund of intellectual pride in Berengar.

out clearly the limits of this study. That Berengar held unorthodox views on the Eucharist seems to have become widely known as early as 1047-1048. At about this time, an old friend of Berengar, Adelmann of Liége, who had studied with Berengar under Fulbert at Chartres, wrote him a mild and solicitous letter, to which he received a scornful reply. Other literature appeared between 1048 and 1060: letters and treatises were written by Hugh, Bishop of Langres, Ascelin of Chartres, Wolphelm of Brauweiler, Theoduin of Liége, Anastasius, a monk of Cluny, and Durand, the abbot of Troarn.[2] The tracts and letters of these early opponents of Berengar are valuable for the history of the controversy; but with the exception of that of Durand they are quite short and tentative in character, and contain nothing which is not better expressed by the greater writers of the second stage of the controversy. They will not enter into this study.

Our direct knowledge of the teaching of Berengar is derived from four sources: some early correspondence; extracts surviving from a short, lost *opusculum,* written shortly after the Roman Council of 1059, cited by Lanfranc in his own treatise which is a reply to this lost opusculum; the lengthy *De sacra coena,* a polemic against Lanfranc, written after Lanfranc's treatise had appeared and before 1079;[3] and finally, a

---

2 Adelmann, *De Eucharistiae sacramento ad Berengarium epistola,* Heurtevent, op. cit., Appendix 2, pp. 287 ff. (Berengar's reply is in Martène and Durand, *Thesaurus novus anecdotarum,* Paris, 1717, 4: 109-113); Hugh, *Tractatus de corpore et sanguine Christi contra Berengarium,* PL 142: 1321-1331; Ascelin, *Epistola ad Berengarium,* PL 150: 66 (Berengar's reply is in the same place); Wolphelm, *Epistola de sacramento Eucharistiae contra errores Berengarii,* PL 154: 414; Theoduin, *Ad Henricum regem contra Brunonem et Berengarium epistola, De corpore et sanguine Domini,* PL 146: 1439-1442; Anastasius, *Epistola ad Giraldum abbatem, De veritate corporis et sanguinis Christi Domini,* PL 149: 433-436; Durand, *Liber de corpore et sanguine Christi contra Berengarium et ejus sectatores,* PL 149: 1375-1424.

3 It is necessary to note this detail of chronology if we are to understand the precise nature of the personal struggle between Berengar and Lanfranc. The treatise of Lanfranc was written about 1066-1069, not in reply to the *De Sacra coena,* which had not yet been written, but to the lost *opusculum;* and the *De sacra coena* is in turn a reply to Lanfranc. In our own study, however, we will not be bound by that chronology, but will develop the teaching of Berengar before that of Lanfranc, citing in the main the *De sacra coena.* This inversion of chronological order is justifiable, since no radical change took place in Berengar's views between the date of the lost *opusculum* and that of the *De sacra coena,* but only a development in his own understanding of them. The *De sacra coena* represents the thought of Berengar in its achieved form.

The edition used in this study is the following: *Berengarii Turonensis de sacra coena adversus Lanfrancum liber posterior,* (edd. A. F. and F. Th. Vischer), Berlin, 1834. A new edition of the *De sacra coena,* by W. H. Beekenkamp, Coll. Kerichistorische studien, Dee I.'s Gravenhage, Nyhoff, 1941, was not available for this study. According to the review of De Ghellinck, *Nouvelle revue théologique,* 68 (1946) 359-360, this Beekenkamp edition has not eliminated all of the difficulties of the Vischer edition.

brief memorial of the events of 1078-1079, written by Berengar shortly after the Roman Council of 1079.[4]

The great work of Berengar is the *De sacra coena,* an extremely rare book, edited in its entirety only once (until the appearance of the Beekenkamp edition of 1941), since the discovery in 1770 of the only extant manuscript. Considered entirely apart from the doctrine which it presents, the *De sacra coena* is a wretched book, extremely lengthy and prolix, written in abominable Latin without any semblance of order or consecutive development, a solid block of 290 octavo pages in the Vischer edition of 1834, without a single heading, often trailing along for pages on end without so much as a paragraph division, and worst of all, made entirely tedious by the constant repetition of its themes—one often feels he is reading over and over again the same page. But from the very repetitions it is possible to isolate many of Berengar's leading ideas and put them in order.

The three great works of anti-Berengarian controversy are the treatises of Lanfranc of Bec, Guitmund of Aversa, and Alger of Liége.[5]

---

4 This last source has been edited by Martène and Durand, *Thesaurus novus anecdotarum,* 4: 103-109.

5 Lanfranc, *De corpore et sanguine Domini adversus Berengarium Turonensem,* PL 150: 407-442. Lanfranc (ca. 1005-1089) was born at Pavia, studied humanities and law, and practiced as an advocate at Pavia; about 1035 he went to France, and for a time taught in the schools at Avranches and later at Rouen. In 1042 he entered the Benedictine monastery at Bec, where he became prior and *scholasticus.* The controversy with Berengar won great acclaim for Lanfranc and his school. In 1059 Duke William of Normandy made him abbot of St. Stephen at Caen. He went with William to Britain in 1066, became Archbishop of Canterbury in 1070, and held that position till his death. His treatise is a polemic work in twenty-three chapters, of which the first seventeen are in dialogue form, between Lanfranc and Berengar, quoting the lost *opusculum.*

Guitmund, *De corporis et sanguinis Christi veritate in Eucharistia, libri tres,* PL 149: 1427-1494; *Sanctorum patrum opuscula selecta* (ed. H. Hurter, S.J.) 38, Innsbruck, 1879. Guitmund was a pupil of Lanfranc at Bec, and monk of the Abbey at Evreaux. The details of his life are obscure. He seems to have gone to England with the Conqueror, and to have been named Archbishop of Rouen, but he never filled the see. He went to Rome, and was named Cardinal and Archbishop of Aversa by Pope Gregory VII. The date of his death is unknown, but there was another Bishop at Aversa in 1095. The *De corpore* was written between 1073-1078. It is a lengthier work than Lanfranc's, also in dialogue form, between Guitmund and a pupil, "Roger."

Alger, *De sacramentis corporis et sanguinis Dominici,* PL 180: 739-854; *Sanctorum patrum opuscula selecta* (ed. H. Hurter, S.J.) 23, Innsbruck, 1873. Alger (ca. 1070-1131), deacon and *scholasticus* of the Chapter of St. Bartholomew at Liége, canon of Liége (1091-1121). About 1121, refusing many offers of preferment, he entered the monastery at Cluny, became a priest there, and died about ten years later. All of his works seem to have been written before he entered Cluny. Besides his Eucharistic work, he is also important in the history of Canon Law. The *De sacramentis* is the longest and best organized work of the three, in three books, of which the third contains material on

Of the three, Lanfranc's is the earliest, and the only one written in direct, personal contact with the adversary. As early as 1049, Berengar wrote a letter to Lanfranc, prior of Bec, friendly and familiar in tone, saying that he had heard from Ingelran of Chartres that Lanfranc rejected the teaching of John the Scot on the Eucharist.[6] He suggested that Lanfranc was not very well versed in the Scriptures, and that if Lanfranc rejected the teaching of John the Scot, he must also hold as heretical the teaching of St. Ambrose, St. Jerome, and St. Augustine, not to mention others.

The reference in the letter to John the Scot makes necessary a brief mention of the background of the controversy. It seems certain that the *Liber Joannis Scoti,* of which Berengar and Lanfranc speak, and which was burned at the Council of Vercelli, is not John the Scot's but the treatise of a ninth century monk of Corbie, Ratramn.[7] This treatise was written in reply to the famous work of Paschasius Radbert, abbot of Corbie, *De corpore et sanguine Domini.* As upon many other points, the Eucharistic ideas of John the Scot are obscure, but he seems to have written no special work on the Eucharist, and he did not figure in the ninth century controversy, except perhaps as a "spectator sympathetic to Ratramn."[9]

It is impossible fully to understand the Berengarian controversy without taking account of its roots in the Radbert-Ratramn controversy of the ninth century. There is no doubt that Berengar based his Eucharistic theology on that of Ratramn, although he thought Ratramn's work to be that of John the Scot; while the adversaries of Berengar followed Paschasius. But this is not to say that the views of Berengar would necessarily have been accepted by Ratramn. The teaching of Ratramn is extremely obscure, and Catholic writers, while not attempting to

6 This letter may be found in Dacher's notes on the life of Lanfranc, PL 150: 63.

7 Ratramnus, *De corpore et sanguine Domini,* PL 121: 103-170.

8 PL 120: 1255-1350.

9 M. Cappuyns, O.S.B., *Jean Scot Erigène, sa vie, son oeuvre, et sa pensée.* Louvain, 1935, p. 91. Cf. Heurtevent, *op. cit.,* Appendix I, pp. 251-285.

the validity of sacraments of the unworthy, entirely untouched by Lanfranc and Guitmund.

Since the titles of these works are so similar, they will henceforth be cited only with the author's name, abbreviated, then volume and column.

Few special studies have been made in recent years of the Eucharistic doctrine of any of these men. One recent work is that of L. Brigué, *Alger de Liége, un théologien de l'eucharistie au debut du XIIe siècle,* Paris, 1936. See a review of this work by Dom Cappuyns, *Bulletin de théologie ancienne et médiévale,* 3 (1937-1940) No. 748.

square Paschasius and Ratramn at every point, generally hold that they can be reconciled in substance.

Similarly, one ought not to speak without qualification of two opposed "currents" of Eucharistic tradition, that of "Ambrosian realism" (St. Ambrose, St. Gregory, Paschasius, Haymo of Halberstadt, Rathier of Verona, Lanfranc), and that of "Augustinian symbolism" (St. Augustine, St. Isidore, John the Scot, Raban Maur, and Berengar). To say that the Augustinian "current" favored a symbolical presence, while the Ambrosian "current" favored a real presence, is an oversimplification, an attempt to read into earlier literature the subject matter of later controversies. No one would hold that the two great western Fathers were opposed in their Eucharistic teaching; and if later writers cited one or the other of them to support their own views, it is a question of emphasis, of the direction of their thought, and of the purpose of their work.[10]

To return, then, to the letter of Berengar to Lanfranc, the latter's account of the history of the letter is interesting on account of the information it gives us of his personal relations with Berengar. According to Lanfranc, when the letter was delivered at Bec, he was not there to receive it, having already gone to Rome to see the Pope, perhaps to attend the Council, perhaps on other business. At any rate, the Council of 1050, concerned with the teachings of Berengar, was then in progress, and Lanfranc took part in its discussions. Meanwhile, at Bec the letter was handed over to "some clerics" for delivery to Lanfranc at Rome. They opened and read it on the way, turned it over to some officials, and to Lanfranc's surprise it was publicly read in the Council. He says then that some doubt was raised about his own orthodoxy, since he had received so familiar a letter from a heretic, and he was called upon to express his own views, which he did to the satisfaction of all.[11] In the *De sacra coena* Berengar ridiculed this story, saying with some justice that he found it difficult to believe the contents of the letter were such as to incriminate Lanfranc; but at the Council the writings of John the Scot (Ratramn) were condemned, Berengar was excommunicated, and an antagonism between the two men was established which was to endure for almost twenty years.

---

10 On this important question, see F. Vernet, "L'eucharistie du XIe à la fin du XIe siècle," DTC 5: 1222-1223. Cf. Heurtevent, *op. cit.*, pl. 168, n. 1, and M. de la Taille, *Mysterium Fidei*, Paris, 1924, p. 407, n. 1.

11 Lanf. PL 150: 413.

Lanfranc took part in various anti-Berengarian discussions in France during the 1050s, and sometime after 1059 wrote his treatise against the *opusculum* which Berengar had written soon after the Roman Council of that year had condemned him once more.[12] Lanfranc seems to have dropped Berengar shortly after his own treatise was written, and to have devoted the rest of his life to ecclesiastical affairs. There is no existing indication that he ever read the *De sacra coena,* which was an attack on him.

The treatises of Guitmund and Alger are entirely lacking in the spirit of personal polemic which marked the work of Lanfranc and Berengar. They are much longer than Lanfranc's, more complete, make freer use of the dialectical method, and claim to take account of subtleties and refinements which grew out of the original error.[13] But the classification together of these three writers, Lanfranc, Guitmund, and Alger, is traditional, going back to the tribute of Peter the Venerable, abbot of Cluny in the twelfth century: concerning the Body of the Lord, Lanfranc had written *bene, plene, perfecte;* Guitmund *melius, plenius, perfectius;* and Alger *optime, plenissime, perfectissime.*[14]

In the remaining part of our study, therefore, we shall attempt to compare and contrast the ideas of Berengar and of his Catholic opponents. We shall study first their theological principles, their general method of procedure, their attitude towards the authority of Scripture and Tradition, and of the Church, and their opinions of the proper place of dialectics in theological science. It was at this deep level of principle that issue was really joined; and the controversy over the substantial conversion and the nature of the sacrament, the two great aspects of Eucharistic theology involved, flowed directly out of their theological principles. We shall study Lanfranc, Guitmund, and Alger not separately, in distinct sections, but compositely, showing among them relationship, dependence, and development. Nor shall we study them directly in the light of their patrology, but rather in that of the

---

12 The Migne edition of Lanfranc carries an account of the final Council of 1079, and the profession of faith imposed upon Berengar at that time. This is an interpolation, and probably represents an addition to the original work made after 1079 by Lanfranc himself. According to Macdonald, *Lanfranc, A Study of His Life, Work, and Writing,* London, 1944, the treatise of Lanfranc was written after 1059 and before 1062, when Lanfranc went to Caen, where his sojourn was too broken by other work to have allowed time for it.

13 Guit, PL. 149: 1430 CD: Alg, Prologue, PL. 180: 739 D - 739 C.

14 Petrus Venerabilis, *Epistola sive tractatus contra Petrobusianos,* PL. 189: 789 CD.

specific contributions which dialectical reasoning permitted them to make to the theology of the Eucharist. In this way we should arrive at a better understanding of the Catholic reply to the first clear-cut Eucharistic heresy in the history of dogma; and we shall see in our writers the high point of Catholic thought at the dawn of scholasticism.

1. *General Characteristics of Procedure*

The theological method of Berengar of Tours is marked by an intensely personal and individualistic approach. In the *De sacra coena* he almost invariably introduces doctrinal assertions with the term, "Ego inquio." It may be argued that this personal approach is to be expected in a work of this kind, a treatise of personal polemic against Lanfranc; yet it is noteworthy that Lanfranc himself never bases doctrinal assertions on his own personal authority nor advances them as his own opinions, but rather states them either impersonally, as the faith of the Church, or in the first person plural, as the universal belief of Catholics.[15] Berengar claims for himself, as a gift of God, a special inward apprehension of the truth, and asserts that he was the only man of wisdom among the madmen who condemned him.[16] There is an abundance of personal invective on both sides of the controversy; it can be found in Lanfranc and to some extent in Guitmund, though the later work of Alger is entirely free from it. But it is safe to say that Berengar outdoes all of his opponents in personal abuse: the word *vecordia*, "madness," appears on almost every page of the *De sacra coena*.

Concerning the necessity of faith as fundamental approach to the Mystery of Faith, Berengar has little to say. The necessity of faith receives no special treatment in the *De sacra coena*, if indeed any subject may be said to have received special treatment in a work so poorly organized. The response of faith, in the sense of an assent of the mind

---

15 Lanf. PL 150: 419 A: "Confitetur enim Ecclesia . . ." 427 C: "Sic enim credimus . . ." 430 C: "Credimus igitur terrenas substantias . . ."

16 *De sacra coena* (henceforth: D.s.c.) p. 74: "Sed quidquid scribas tu . . . indigne nomine vomitus aut volutabri, sed non indignum nomine perceptionis, donante patre misericordiarum, intimae veritatis." Both Lanfranc and Guitmund have noted this individualism in Berengar's theology, and the gnostic tendency which it represents. Lanf. PL 150: 412 B: ". . . verum hanc lucem [fidei] tenebrosa mens tua nequit comprehendere, despectis caeteris, putans se solam sapientem esse." Guit, PL 149: 1428 D: ". . . maluit esse sub aliqua admiratione hominum haereticus, quam sub oculis Dei private vivere Catholicus."

D.s.c., p. 74: ". . . concilio dixisse non nesciam: compressus indoctorum grege conticui, veritus, ne merito haberer insanus, si sapiens inter insanos videri contenderem."

to the existence of an objective Eucharistic reality, does not appear in Berengar's treatise at all; and if he mentions the virtue of faith in passing, it is only with reference to the disposition of the faithful recipient entering into the symbolic meaning of the sacrament. Berengar ridicules the notion of any miracle connected with the Eucharist, not merely in the sense of a subjective appearance of real flesh upon the altar, but also in that of a change of elements. Such a miracle would be unworthy of God.[17] There is not the slightest Scriptural warrant for understanding any miraculous occurrence to have taken place in the Eucharist.[18]

Between the procedure of Berengar and that of his Catholic opponents the contrast is extreme. He had laughed at faith, they assert, had tried to comprehend everything by reason.[19] For them, on the other hand, the sacrament of the altar is above all the "Mystery of Faith."[20] There are areas of the Eucharistic reality which are wholly impenetrable to reason, and can only be humbly believed. The Eucharist is a network of mysteries. It is a fact that Christ is received on earth, yet He remains whole and entire in heaven. It is a fact that bread is changed into His Body, and wine into His Blood, and that the nature of the elements undergoes a change. But if the manner be sought through which these marvels are accomplished, the response must be, "The just man, who lives by faith, does not seek to pry into his faith with arguments, nor to grasp it with his reason."[21] In his insistence on the impenetrability of the sacrament to rational inquiry, Lanfranc indeed sealed off from the investigation certain questions which actually did lie within the field of legitimate rational speculation, and thus left to

---

17 *Ibid.*, p. 96: "Per miraculum dicis ista fieri, admirationi debere; verius dixisses ad iniuriam et contemptum dei."

18 *Ibid.*, p. 97: "Vere dicitur angelum satane in angelum se lucis transfigurare quia dixisti, quasi non contra veritatem per miraculum ista fieri; da de propheta, de apostolo. de evangelista locum aliquem, unde manifestissimum sit, . . ."

19 Lanf. PL 150: 427 B: ". . . fidem arridere, rationibus omnia velle comprehendere."

20 *Ibid.*, 421 D: "Si quaeris modum quo id fieri potest, breviter ad praesens respondeo: Mysterium fidei credi salubriter potest, vestigari utiliter non potest."
Guit. PL 149: 1439 B: "Nam et ipse Dominus noster Jesus Christus sacramenta haec, mysterium fidei appellavit. Ut quid ergo mysterium, nisi quia occultum? Ut quid fidei, nisi quod hoc non carnis oculo, sed intuitu fidei convenit comtemplari?"

21 Lanf. PL 150: 427 A: "Quonammodo panis efficiatur caro vinumque convertatur in sanguinem, utriusque essentialiter mutata natura, justus, qui ex fide vivit, scrutari argumentis et concipere ratione non quaerit."
Cf. Alg. PL 180: 820 D: "Quod quia ineffabile est, quomodo corpus Christi hic fiat, et ibi manet, ad intelligentiam spiritualem et fidem talia cogitantes revocat, qui etsi sciri non potest, credi potest."

others the development of fields which he did not dare to touch. Lanfranc's hesitancies will appear from time to time in this study.

In the view of the opponents of Berengar, the Eucharist has been given by God to mankind in such a mysterious form precisely in order that we may have the opportunity to exercise our faith, and thus more surely attain to the reward of faith.[22] The test of faith is to hold strongly to the revealed truth, even though it be contrary to the evidence of sense, even though it be beyond the capacity of the intelligence to grasp; this acceptance is indeed an agony for our minds, but the grace of God makes it possible.[23] For what merit would there be for us if everything in the Eucharist were visible?—visible miracles are not for the faithful, but for infidels.[24] As Lanfranc says,

> The faithful Catholic prefers to approach the heavenly mysteries by faith, so as to be able finally to attain to faith's reward, than without faith to waste time laboring to understand things which cannot be understood; since he knows that it is written: "Seek not the things that are too high for thee. . . ." (Eccl. 3:22)[25]

The prologue of Alger's treatise is given over almost entirely to exhortations to faith. A catalogue of the mysteries involved in the Catholic doctrine of the Eucharist is closed with the words, "But these things hidden to reason are manifest to faith."[26] Alger's work is characterized by a beauty of style and emotional appeal which are lacking in the more arid and more controversial treatises of Lanfranc and Guitmund— one of the good reasons, doubtless, why Peter the Venerable awarded the palm to the *scholasticus* of Liége among the opponents of Berengar. Consequently, his appeals to faith in the Eucharist are graceful and winning. He argues from the grades of perfection among creatures: we surpass the beasts and are not understood by them; so God in-

---

22 Guit., PL 149: 1439 A: "Atque ita quandiu in agone fidei certamus, quandiu peregrinamur a Domino, fidem nostram sedulo convenit exerceri, quatenus exercendo erudiatur, erudiendo pascatur, pascendo augeatur, augendo perficiatur, perfecta coronetur."

23 Alg. 820 D: "Sicque dum exteriorum sensuum testimonio non acquiescit, nec interiore inquisitione comprehendus, de veritate non titubat; fit per Dei gratiam, ut in tali suo agone fides nostra exerceatur. . . ."

24 Guit. 1439 A: "Denique manifesta miracula non propter fideles, sed propter infideles."

25 Lanf. 427 A: ". . . mavult enim coelistibus mysteriis fidem adhibere, ut ad fidei praemia valeat quandoque pervenire, quam fide omissa in comprehendis iis, quae comprehendi non possunt, supervacue laborare, sciens scriptum esse: Altiora te ne quaesieris. . . . (Eccl. 3:22)."

26 Alg. 741 B: "Sed haec rationi caeca, fidei sunt manifestata."

finitely surpasses us, and we cannot hope to understand his designs.[27]
He argues from the interdependence of the senses of the body. The
eye apprehends color, the ear is responsive to sound. The ear does not
see the wagon pass, the eye does not hear the rumble of its wheels—
are there, therefore, no wagon and no sound? Does the whole world
not exist because we do not see all of it at once? Just as our senses
ought not to judge each other, so our intellect ought not to judge of
that which is incomprehensible to it.[28]

And finally, with regard to the question of faith, Guitmund lays
down as basic principle of the Catholic approach to the Eucharist the
famous dictum of St. Augustine, the *credo ut intelligam,* which was to
become the charter of developed scholasticism in the mind of St.
Anselm. As Guitmund puts it:

> For Christ did not command you to understand, but to believe. His
> is the care how that be done which He wishes to be done. Yours is not
> to discuss, but humbly to believe. . . . For you do not understand that
> later you may believe; you believe in order afterwards to understand.[29]

And since the opponents of Berengar approach the Eucharist from
the viewpoint of the common faith of the Church, in contrast to Berengar's intense personalism, we may expect to find in them a more objective method. It has already been remarked that their judgments are
not presented as personal opinions, but as the faith of the Church. Their
attitude is that of men setting forth a belief not of their own making—
a belief which they are convinced will exist forever whether they defend
it or not—hence we see in their writing a serene lucidity far different
from the "Ego inquio" and turgid repetitions of Berengar.

Consequently, when our authors make a statement of the method
which they intend to pursue, they say they will appeal to authority as
well as to reason.[30] When Alger takes up the "new and absurd" error
of impanationism, he says it is to be destroyed at the root, through

---

27 *Ibid.,* 742 A.

28 Alg. 742 D: "Ut sicut illa incomprehensibilia sunt sensibus non minus esse cre-
duntur, sic quae sunt incomprehensibilia intellectibus humanis non minus esse credantur."

29 Guit. 1441 C: "Non enim praecepit tibi Christus: Intellige, sed crede. Ejus est
curare quomodo id quod fieri vult, fiat tuum est autem non discutere, sed humiliter credere, quia quidquid omnino fieri vult, fiat. Non enim intelligendum est, ut postmodum
credas: sed prius credendum, ut postmodum intelligas."

30 Lanf. 414 B: ". . . de hac re opportunius tibi respondebo, cum fidem hanc,
auctore Deo, divinis auctoribus et manifestis rationibus veram esse monstravero."

reason and authority.[31]   When at Rome in 1050 Lanfranc was called upon to express his own convictions regarding the Holy Eucharist, he tells us that he was instructed to do so "more by means of sacred authorities than by arguments."[32]

In the third book of Guitmund's treatise, there is an example of pre-scholastic theological method at its highest point, where it was about to enter into scholasticism proper.   Guitmund sets down first the statement of his theological principles, the *loci theologici* on which he means to build, and the *status quaestionis;* [33] then the proofs;[34] and finally the conclusion to the whole treatise in the form of a syllogism.[35]

2. *Scripture and Tradition*

Despite the extremely personal character of his method, Berengar professed the highest regard for the authority of Scripture and Tradition.   He lays it down as a principle that the Holy Spirit speaks in Scripture.[36]   Scripture is the sovereign authority which one must not oppose; the Holy Scriptures are endowed with the inescapable weight of authority.[37]   But it is not enough simply to know and repeat the texts : one must be endowed with sufficient perception to be able to extract from them their meaning.   The Scriptures abound in figurative language, which demands a spiritual and not a carnal interpretation.   If the Holy Scriptures are interpreted in the physical sense, they no longer nourish but destroy, since there is in the Gospel a letter that kills.[38]

---

31 Alg. 754 B: "Quae haeresis, quia nova et absurda est, rationibus et auctoritatibus, prout Deus aspiraverit, radicitus est exstirpanda."

32 Lanf. 413 B. "Post haec praecepit papa [Leo IX, at Council of Rome, 1050] ut ego surgerem, pravi rumoris a me maculam abstergerem, fidem meam exponerem, expositam plus sacris auctoritatibus quam argumentis probarem."

33 Guit. 1469 AB: 1) "consuetudo catholicae fidei;" 2) "de sanctis scripturis [including Tradition] ; 3) "propria argumenta."
Ibid., 1) "corpus Christi verum in substantia sua, non in umbra Berengariana;" 2) "contra impanatores."

34 *Ibid.,* 1469-1488: 1) from Tradition; 2) from miracles; 3) from liturgy; 4) from the authority of the Church; 5) from reason; the Catholic doctrine is established by demonstration that the position of the "umbratici" and the "impanatores" is absurd.

35 *Ibid.,* 1489 CD.

36 D.s.c., p. 161.

37 *Ibid.,* p. 57: ". . . non mea, non tua sed evangelica apostolicaque simul autenticarum scripturarum, quibus contra ire fas non sit."
Ibid., p. 245: "Dum enim dicis, absumi panem in altari per corruptionem subjecti . . . contra propheticae, evangelicae, ut caeteros taceam, indeclinabile pondus auctoritatis."

38 *Ibid.,* p. 270: "Agnoscite, quia figurae sunt, quae in divinis voluminibus scripta sunt, ideo tamquam spirituales et non carnales intelligite, quae dicuntur."
Ibid., "Si enim quasi carnales ista suscipitis, laedunt vos, non alunt; est enim in evangeliis litera, quae occidat."

For Berengar then, the Bible is a rule of faith of the highest authority, but it is not of exclusive or even of final authority; its data must be tested in the light of some standard which is itself non-Scriptural; and the precise determination of what that standard is to be lies at the heart of the Berengarian theology.[39]

It would be false to assert that Berengar attempted to build up a system of Eucharistic theology without reference to the tradition of the Fathers. He replies to Lanfranc's reproach that he has little re-spect for traditional authority by saying that this is a lie: he has used the sacred authorities in framing his argument wherever there was a need.[40] As we saw in the letter to Lanfranc of 1049, he claimed from the earliest days of the controversy that his teaching had the support of the Fathers, especially of St. Augustine and St. Ambrose. It is not difficult for us to see how he might have claimed the patronage of St. Augustine, since his theory of the nature of the sacrament is simply the Augustinian teaching of the sign, pushed to a limit which would ex-clude any objective presence of Christ's Body under the Eucharistic spe-cies. But his affection for St. Ambrose is harder to explain, since the writings of this Father contain unmistakeably the doctrine of sub-stantial conversion. Yet if it is a fact that both Fathers are cited abundantly in the *De sacra coena*, it is also true that St. Ambrose ap-pears even more often than St. Augustine. It may be that Berengar realized that he was faced with a special problem in St. Ambrose, and wished to meet it as well as he could.

In his treatment of St. Ambrose, therefore, Berengar is extremely selective, choosing only passages which seem to support his theory and rejecting the rest, or twisting the meaning of passages which seem to bear against him. Thus, for example, he introduces a strained and tortuous dialectical discussion of an unmistakeably "realist" text of St. Ambrose in the *De mysteriis* with the following admission:

---

39 Cf. Macdonald, *op. cit.*, p. 219, where he gives us an advance hint to the nature of the Berengarian standard of interpretation: "When we estimate his contribution to the progress of the Evangelical principle, we shall find it not so much in the appeal to Scripture as the final authority for belief — although he never loses an opportunity to quote the Bible — but in the demand for freedom whereby the individual may open the books of Scripture and there judge for himself the meaning of God's word. The Evangelical principle of the freedom of private judgment was originated in the Middle Ages by Berengar."

40 D.s.c., p. 100: "Manifestum fiet, divinitate propitia, illud de calumnia scribere te, non de veritate, ubi deducendi sacras auctoritates in medium necessitate inde agendi locus occurerit."

With these premises, the passage must be understood to bear against you, even though certain expressions [of St. Ambrose] are so obscure that it is difficult or even impossible for me to interpret them according to a norm of manifest meaning.[41]

But the Archdeacon of Angers felt that he was on stronger ground when he came to deal with an ambiguous text of the *De sacramentis*:

You see, therefore, how effective is the word of Christ. If then, there is so much power in Christ's word that things should begin to exist which did not exist at all, how much more effective is it that they should remain what they were and be changed into something else?[42]

The ambiguity, of course, is in the last phrase, "that they should remain what they were and be changed into something else." Berengar interpreted the passage to mean that the Eucharistic elements remain what they are substantially, but acquire a new religious value through consecration; just as the water of Baptism does not cease to be water, but acquires the *virtus Christi* through the consecration of the priest. And

---

41 *Ibid.*, p. 176: "His praefixis, illud contra te oportet intendi, etiam si nonulla extent ita obscura ut difficile vel impossibile sit mihi, ad normam manifestorum interpretari."

The peculiar elliptical phrase, *ad normam ea manifestorum interpretari*, is characteristic of Berengar. It has been translated here, "according to a norm of manifest meaning." Justification of that translation will be made in an important context, *infra*, pp. 58-59.

The "obscure" passage of St. Ambrose in question is that from the *De mysteriis*, 9, (J. Quasten, ed., *Monumenta eucharistica et liturgica vetustissima*, part 3, *Florilegium Patristicum tam veteris quam medii aevi auctores complectens*, Fasc. 7, Bonn, 1936, pp. 133-134: "Forte dicas: Aliud video, quomodo tu mihi adseris, quod Christi corpus accipiam? Et hoc nobis adhuc superest ut probemus. Quantis igitur utimur exemplis? Probemus non hos esse, quod natura formavit, sed quod benedictio consecravit, maioremque vim esse benedictionis quam naturae; quia benedictione etiam natura ipsa mutatur." And the rest of the chapter.

Even a writer so favorable to Berengar as Macdonald has noted Berengar's attempt "to twist the Ambrosian realism to support his own interpretation" (*op. cit.*, p. 327). J. Schnitzer, *Berengar von Tours, sein Leben und seine Lehre*, Stuttgart, 1892, p. 291, analyzes Berengar's dialectical handling of this Ambrosian passage.

42 St. Ambrose, *De sacramentis*, 4, 4, J. Quasten, *op. cit.*, p. 159: "Vides ergo quam operatorius sit sermo Christi. Si ergo tanta vis est in sermone Domini Jesu, ut inciperent esse, quae non erant, quanto magis operatorius est, ut sint, quae erant, et in aliud commutentur?"

Cf. Lanfranc's suggested reading of the text, PL 150: 420 D - 421 A: "In quibusdam tamen codicibus praefata sententia verbis aliis invenitur hoc modo: 'Si igitur tanta vis est in sermone Domini Jesus ut inciperent esse quae non erant, quanto magis operatorius est ut quae erant in aliud commutentur'?" A suggestion repeated by P. Battifol, *Etudes d'histoire et de théologie positive*, 2nd series, Paris, 1905, p. 104. But the text is correct.

he assails the contrary interpretation of Lanfranc.[43]   Then in reply
to Lanfranc's accusation that he has twisted the meaning by taking the
passage out of its context,[44] he is compelled to admit that he has not
cited Ambrose verbatim, but claims he has cited him only partially for
the sake of brevity.[45]

The discussion between Lanfranc and Berengar of the ambiguous
text of the *De sacramentis* brings out clearly the radical opposition between the two men in their approach to tradition.   Lanfranc rightly insists that the passage should be placed in its context,[46] and points out
that any but a realist interpretation of the text would contradict previous
expressions in the same chapter; while Berengar seizes upon the text because it seems to provide some support for his own view, and then discusses it in isolation from the rest.   Lanfranc has astutely noted this
characteristic of the Berengarian exegesis, and has put his finger on the
radical source of it.[47]   And Macdonald agrees that Lanfranc's criticism
is correct.[48]

The reliance of the anti-Berengarian writers on the tradition of the
Fathers was enormous.   In this aspect of their teaching is brought out
that objectivity which was their great aim.   Perhaps they had been so
impressed by the novelty inherent in the ideas of Berengar that they
were doubly anxious to avoid giving the impression of interpreting the
divine word "according to their own sense."[49]   The witness of tradition
is added to the words of Christ because often His own words do not

---

43 D.s.c., pp. 180-181: "Scribis enim in eo, quod dicit beatus Ambrosius: si operatorius est Christi sermo ut inciperent esse quae non erant, multo magis operatorius est,
ut sint quae erant, et in aliud commutentur, subaudiri oportere: specie, ut ita legatur: ut
sint specie. Si dissimulare volueris, hoc te dixisse contra eruditionem tuam, admirationem
facis."

44 Lanf. PL 150: 420 C: ". . . perspicaciter agnoscat qua fraude fingis non inventa; qua astutia depravis inventa qua pervicacia in illud detorquere conaris quaecum-
que relinquis illaesa."

45 D.s.c., p. 184: ". . . quod facere manifestum non possem, si dans operam brevi-
tati objectionem, quam sibi beatus Ambrosius fieri voluit, totiusque ad objecta responsi-
onis non prosequerer seriem."

46 Lanf. 420 B: "Sextum quoque De sacramentis librum in quo opere praefatum
mendacium eum dixesse medaciter affirmasti, sic incipit. . .. "

47 *Ibid.*, 408 AB: ". . . sententias . . . sacris doctoribus attribuis dicens: Hoc vel
hoc in illo, seu illo opere testatur Augustinus, Gregorius, Hieronymus. . . . Ibi enim
conquiesceret omnis versuta tergiversatio . . . quae de Scripturis sanctis te sumere non-
numquam dicis; aut penitus esse falsa, aut aliqua ex parte, *prout ratio tui negotii postu-
lat,* depravata."

48 *Op. cit.*, p. 324: "[Berengar] contends that the doctrine of a change of essence
does not appear in the teaching of that writer [Ambrose], yet he was only able to arrive
at that conclusion by a partial use of his own principle of interpretation. He selects
Ambrosian statements which are relevant to his own theory and disregards the rest."

49 Alg. PL 180: 776 C: ". . . ne meo sensu interpretari videar, exponit Augustinus
in sermone 27 super Joannem. . . ."

carry their own explanation: sometimes He spoke literally, sometimes figuratively, though always truly. He distinguished among His auditors: to some it was given to understand the mystery of the Kingdom of God, to others only in parables.[50] And if the saints found it not a useless task to write at length upon the Scriptures, we ought not find it useless to study their interpretations. For the more certainly the Christian faith is known, the more useful it becomes; and the testimony of authority lends greater certitude to our knowledge.[51] The witness of the Fathers is of the greatest value to confirm faith and to desroy heresy.[52] The two principles which must be followed in interpreting patristic literature are, first, that obscure texts are to be interpreted in the light of clearer texts;[53] and second, that the entire context of the author must be used.[54] Both of these principles are in marked contrast to the practice of Berengar already noted of cutting the patristic teachings to suit his own notions. A third principle that the Fathers be interpreted in accordance with the authority of the teaching Church, will be discussed separately.

It must be confessed that the patrology of our authors is marred by improper citations and the attribution of apocryphal matter to Fathers of the Church.[55] One of the most curious instances of this sort of error in scholarship is that of Alger attributing to St. Augustine, "in libro sententiarum Prosperi," a text of Lanfranc which Alger must have read, without attribution to St. Augustine, in Lanfranc's own work.[56] Mis-

---

50 *Ibid.*, 777 C: "Testimonio Christi testes alios adhibere praesumpsi; sed quia ipse quidem semper vere, aliquando tamen loquitur proprie, aliquando figurate, auditoresque suos ita discrevit, ut his datum sit nosse mysterium regni Dei, caeteris autem in parabolis. . . ."

51 *Ibid.*, "Quod ipsis sanctis non pigrum fuit scribere, necessarium duxi repetere; ut ipse intellectus, veritatis non meae videatur praesumptionis, sed catholicae auctoritatis, eorum qui crediderunt, et ita salvari meruerunt; quia fides Christiana quo fit certior, eo est utilior. Ut ergo certior sit, aliorum sanctorum subdatur auctoritas."

52 Guit., PL 149: 1469 AB: "Sed quoniam et valde multa ad roborandas adhuc partes nostras, et adversariorum diruendas, Deo adjuvante, addi possunt . . . de sanctis Scripturis adhuc aliqua proferemus. . . ."

53 Lanf. PL 150: 419 D: "Et quidem si de sacramentis seu caeteris de quibus Ambrosius scripsit omnes revolvas libros quos Ecclesia in usu nunc habet, tale aliquid ab Ambrosio dictum, taliterque expositum nusquam reperire valebit. . . . Accipe potius quid in libro De mysteriis sive initiandis dicat."

54 Alg., 757 A: "Ut videamus B. Ambrosium sibi vel aliis sanctis non esse contrarium, verba sua in ordine suo ponamus."

55 See M. Lepin, *L'Idée du sacrifice de la Messe, d'aprés les théologiens, depuis l'origine jusqu'à nos jours*, 2nd. ed., Paris, 1926, Appendix, pp. 759 ff., for examples of this. Paschasius Radbert is often cited as St. Augustine. Faustus of Rietz is invariably cited under the name of Eusebius of Emessa, and the treatise of St. John Chrysostom on the priesthood is attributed to St. Basil.

56 Alg., 792 D. Lanf., 424 A.

takes of this sort were common during the early Middle Ages. In his preface to the Migne edition of Alger, Malou writes that we ought readily to condone Alger's mistakes: books were scarce in his time, and besides, Alger never proffers apocryphal testimonies without at the same time fully and acutely establishing his position upon genuine sources.[57]

If the patristic documentation of our authors is rich, their use of Scripture is rather scanty. As Turmel writes, "In his attack on the doctrine of the real presence, or at least that of transubstantiation, (Berengar) had appealed principally to the weapons of sense, of reason, and of tradition. As it happens always, the defense was modelled on the attack . . . All those who rallied to refute the heresiarch placed themselves almost exclusively upon the double terrain of tradition and of reason."[58] There are, however, short Scriptural arguments in all of them. When Lanfranc is about to go forward with his positive proof of the doctrine of the substantial change, he sets down first his argument from Scripture, based upon the words of institution,[59] but only a few uncommented lines are given to it, followed by pages of patristic argument. Guitmund has a short commentary on the pronoun "hoc" of the words of institution. The heretics claimed it to be a relative pronoun denoting the substance considered independently of accidents. Against them, Guitmund alleges the authority of the "dialecticians" and of Donatus for his position that the pronoun does not relate to any determined substance, but is merely demonstrative.[60] Again Guitmund calls on the words of institution against the impanationists:

Christ said: "This is My Body." He did not say: "In this My Body lies concealed." He did not say: "In this wine is My Blood," but He said: "This is My Blood."[61]

And finally, Alger gives us what is rare among these writers, a short commentary on the words of institution in the form of a paraphrase.[62]

---

57 J. B. Malou, PL 180: 735.

58 J. Turmel, *Histoire de la théologie positive, depuis l'origine jusqu'à Concile de Trente,* 3rd. ed., Paris, 1904, p. 310.

59 Lanf., 439 D.

60 Guit., 1467 A: "Hoc enim pronomen non est ad supradicta relativum sed tantummodo demonstrativum." Cf. 1436 BC.

61 *Ibid.,* 1484 C: ". . . ait [Christus]: *Hoc est corpus meum.* Non ait: In hoc latet corpus meum. Nec dixit: In hoc vino est sanguis meus, sed dixit: Hic est sanguis meus."

62 Alg., PL 180: 776 A: "Non futurum praedico, non absens aliquid denuntio, sed hoc quod praesentialiter do, est corpus meum, non figuratum, sed verum, ipsum quod pro vobis tradetur. Hic est sanguis meus, idem ipse, qui pro nobis effundetur, addens etiam proprie proprium suae carnis et sanguinis effectum, scilicet in remissionem peccatorum."

3. *Authority of the Church.*

Upon the principle of the authority of Scripture and tradition, Berengar and his opponents were at least in verbal agreement, though they differed widely in their application of the principle. But upon the question of the *magisterium* of the church, which is the proximate rule of faith, their positions were flatly contradictory. Berengar had nothing but contempt for the *magisterium*, whether its authority was brought to bear on him in a general way, through the common consent of the faithful—the authority of the *ecclesia discens*—or in a particular way, in the Councils of the *ecclesia docens* which were called to deal specifically with his teachings. It was inevitable that his independent and individualistic spirit would clash with a belief that was popular, and with formulas which were imposed on him in the name of authority.

In the first place, the faith of Catholics, the common consent of the faithful, is itself a norm by which the true import of Catholic tradition may be discovered. Berengar knew the faith of the Church: it was everywhere around him, it was in the air he breathed. But to say to him that his teachings contradicted the universal belief of Catholics was to say nothing at all. "Why be wrong with all the world," he would have answered, "if all the world is wrong?"[63] It is the opinion of Lanfranc, says Berengar, that an idea which has been a matter of routine acceptance is for that reason more probably true; but Lanfranc is wrong in identifying a crowd of fools with the Church.[64] The majority is not always right, he insists, and cites in support of this conclusion the experience of the Church in Africa, where during the heresies of the fourth century, the multitude favored error, while only as few retained the Catholic truth.[65]

Then the Archdeacon transfers to the Councils which dealt with his teachings his contempt for the ineptitude of the crowd. It is a rare

---

63 A. Clerval, *Les Écoles de Chartres*, p. 131: Tout autre [from that of Fulbert] était le méthode de Bérenger. Pour lui, l'autorité ne comptait pas, ni en exégèse, ni en théologie. 'A quoi bon se tromper avec tout le monde,' disait-il un jour, 'si tout le monde se trompe.' "

64 D.s.c., pp. 34-35: "Quod usitatam ecclesiae fidem non dubitas dicere, et, si quae usitatiora, ea debeant esse probabiliora . . . iam dixi superius, ineptorum in ecclesia turbas non esse ecclesiam."

65 *Ibid.*, p. 34: ". . . de multitudine quantacunque quorumcunque superius iam respondi, eam veritati nunquam praejudicare, adversarios Caeciliani multitudinem maximam habuisse . . . non defuisse post illum multitudinem beato in Affrica Cipriano. . . ." An argument which appears with the most tiresome repetition in almost identical terms, in many of the early pages of the *De sacra coena*.

thing indeed to find the majority in possession of the truth; and this incapacity extends as well to Councils of the Church, which lack that inward perception which is necessary for a diligent inquiry into the truth.[66] Lanfranc has called the Council of Rome of 1059 "the Church"—he might better have referred to it as an errant mob. And the Council of Vercelli of 1050 was an assembly of simpletons, a council of vanity, a hubbub.[67]

Not only towards the Councils but also towards the Holy See itself was Berengar lacking both in respect and obedience. Cited by Pope St. Leo IX to appear before the Council of Vercelli, he refused to appear, and gave as his reason the canonical cause that a cleric cannot be summoned before a tribunal outside of his province.[68] He says that at Rome in 1050 he found Pope St. Leo anything but a holy father, not even an honest man; and he applies to the Pope the words of Our Lord condemning the Pharisees, "The father from whom you are is the devil."[69] After the council of Rome in 1059 he composed a written refutation, the pamphlet answered by Lanfranc, in which he sharply attacked the Roman Church and Pope Nicholas II, and in the *De sacra coena* he accused Pope Nicholas of levity, of ignorance, and of un-

---

66 *Ibid.*, p. 59: ". . . vix unquam in multitudine satis bene quaesitam inventamque veritatem; . . . multitudinem non esse idoneam satis ad diligentiorem veritatis inquisitionem atque perceptionem."

67 *Ibid.*, p. 49: " . . . ecclesiae dicis, quod turbae erraticae verius dicere potuisti."

Ibid., p. 43: ". . . concilio vanitatis . . ." p. 44: ". . . ad Vercellicum tumultum illum convenerint."

Cf. Bernold of Constance, PL 148: 1456, Durand of Troarn, PL 149: 1422, Lanfranc, PL 150: 426; 422. In connection with Berengar's attitude towards the Roman Church Harnack has a curious note (*History of Dogma*, vol. 6, transl. from 3rd German edition, W. M'Gilchrist, London, 1899): "With the dialectic there mingle the beginnings of a more independent, a critical view of history. Yet Berengar meddles with no decree of any Council. Only the decrees connected with his subject are ridiculed by him." If Harnack is referring to General Councils, it must be said that the time of Berengar was not the time of General Councils: none had been held since IV Constantinople, in 869; none would be held till I Lateran in 1123. It has already been shown (*supra*, p. 17) that the churchmen of the pre-scholastic centuries had great respect for provincial Councils, especially those presided over by the Pope or his legate, and regarded them as possessing great weight. If Berengar ridiculed only "the decrees connected with his subject," it is because these were the only decrees which might conceivably have concerned him.

68 D.s.c., p. 41: "Pervenerat enim ad me, praecepisse Leonem illum, ut ego Vercellensi illi conventui, in quo tamen nullam papae debebam obedientiam, non deesem. Dissuaserant secundum ecclesiastica iura, secundum quae nullus extra provinciam ad iudicium ire cogendus est, personae ecclesiasticae, dissuaserant amici."

69 *Ibid.*, pp. 33-34: "Ego papam minime sanctam . . . et, ut alterius aliquid audeam secundum illum, qui dixit: vos ex diabolo patre estis, minime virum probum expertus sum." Cf. p. 48.

worthy conduct.[70]   And finally, after the death of Pope Alexander II and the accession of Gregory VII, there came from Rome to Berengar an instruction to keep silence, which did not prevent him from again propounding his views before a synod at Poitiers, in January, 1076.[71]

It is clear, then, that Berengar rejected entirely the authority of the teaching Church as possessing any normative value for discovering the meaning of the message contained in Scripture and tradition. On this account at least, it is now demonstrated that the error of Berengar lay far deeper than a false view merely of Eucharistic doctrine : it attacked one of the foundations of Catholic belief, the living *magisterium* of the Church as proximate rule of faith. In his refusal to allow special authority to the Roman See—indeed, in his avowed contempt for the Roman See—he exceeded all other rationalizing dialecticians of the pre-scholastic period, to whom decision by Rome meant an end of controversy.

Lanfranc observed this fundamental error of Berengar, and marked it as the particular note of his heresy, distinguishing Berengar from the heretics of history. Berengar had given over to contempt the Holy Roman Church, had called it a church of demons, a council of vanity, a seat of Satan. Heretics and schismatics of the past had been guilty of no such impiety as this, says Lanfranc. Even though some might have wandered from the truth and fallen into error, yet all of them had held the see of Peter in the highest honor, nor had any dared to speak or write such blasphemy against it.[72] It is useless for Berengar to assert that the doctrine which he attacks is the opinion of a vulgar mob, and that his own teaching corresponds to that of some ideal Church, for the opinion of Paschasius and Lanfranc is precisely that which has been held by all orders and ranks in the existing Church, with the exception of a few heretics and schismatics.[73] The fact is that Berengar is rejecting not an opinion, but the doctrine of the Catholic Church, and is separating himself from it.[74]

The modern writer, Ebersolt, places this rejection of ecclesiastical authority at the root of the Berengarian doctrine, an attack not merely on the traditional Eucharistic teaching, but at the deeper level of the

---

70 *Ibid.*, p. 71 : ". . . nimiaque levitate Nicolaus ille, de cuius ineruditione et morum indignitate facile mihi non insufficienter scribere."

71 M. Cappuyns, "Bérenger de Tours," DHGE 8: 394.

72 Lanf., PL 150: 426 BC.

73 *Ibid.*, 414 A.

74 *Ibid.*, Cf. 409 C ; 410 B.

foundations of Catholic belief.[75]   And this is indeed true: the Berengarian heresy, seen in its principles, was two-sided, and the rejection of ecclesiastical authority was its negative side.

Upon this question of the authority of the Church, as upon the Eucharistic doctrine itself, the antithesis between the two parties was complete.   Berengar rejected the authority of the Church entirely; for his opponents the authority of the Church was the one great norm to which every interpretation must be adjusted.   The teaching of the Church is the rule of faith.[76]   Berengar had despised the opinion to which he had been forced to submit at Rome in 1059 as that of a vulgar mob; to this Lanfranc replies with a ringing expression of the Catholic spirit:

> When you say, "The Burgundian [Cardinal Humbert] was of the opinion of the mob, of Paschasius and Lanfranc," you are including me also among the mob; now I want you most certainly to know, and my friends and the Church of Christ to believe: I should far prefer to be an oafish and simple-minded Catholic with the crowd than a fastidious and inquisitive heretic with you.[77]

If the teaching authority of the Church is the proximate rule of faith, then more specifically adherence to the Roman Church is the actual test of orthodoxy.[78]   The text from St. Matthew, *Tu es Petrus . . .,* may have a wider application, says Lanfranc, than to the Church at Rome, and it is so held by some Catholic writers; but its principal import is to give special authority to the canons and decrees of the Popes.[79]   Lanfranc, Guitmund, and Alger all cite against Berengar the decrees of the Councils by which he was condemned and the professions of faith

---

75 J. Ebersolt, "Essai sur Bérenger de Tours et la controverse sacramentaire au XIe siècle," *Revue de l'histoire des Religions,* 48 (1903) 163: "[Berengar] donnait ainsi le droit à l'individu de se soustraire à une autorité par amour de la vérité. Bérenger niait par ce fait le dogme de l'infaillibilité. De quel droit en effet l'Église s'est elle arrogé le monopole de la vérité?"

76 Lanf., 407 B: ". . . et ad veram fidem quam sancta Ecclesia praedicare non cessat."

Guit., PL 149: 1469 A. "Quicumque enim vult salvus esse, sicut sancti Patres sanxerunt, et totius concinit mundus, necesse est ut teneat catholicam fidem."

77 Lanf., 414 BC: "Porro autem quod dicis, Erat autum Burgundus in sententia vulgi, Paschasii atque Lanfranci, me etiam cum vulgo deputas, certissimum habeto tu, indubitanter credant amici mei, atque Eccleisa Christi, . . . mallem tamen cum vulgo esse rusticus et idiota Catholicus quam tecum existere curialis atque facetus haereticus."

78 Lanf., 410 B: ". . . haeriticum esse omnem hominem qui a Romana et universali Ecclesia, in fidei doctrina, discordat."

79 *Ibid.,* 426 D: [After citing Mt. 16: 18-19, Tu es Petrus . . .] "Quae tametsi de pastoribus sanctae Ecclesiae dicta esse credantur, et a quibusdam catholicis exponantur, praecipue tamen de Romana ecclesia intelligenda esse sacri canones et pontificum decreta testantur."

which he made before the Councils.[80]   And Lanfranc cites in succession
the Popes who have dealt with the Berengarian heresy.[81]

The Archdeacon of Angers had ridiculed the common belief of
Catholics as in any sense a guarantee of truth; it was a rare thing for
the multitude to possess the truth. Against this gnostic tendency, typ-
ical of heresy, the Catholics allege the universal consent of the faithful
as having a share in the authoritative teaching of the Church. Indeed,
this common consent of itself should be enough to carry conviction
of the truth.[82] The whole Church, in the East and in the West, has
held to one common belief concerning the Eucharist. If such a common
faith should be proved false, then either the Catholic Church has never
existed or it has perished, for an error in belief upon a point of such
magnitude must surely be fatal. But no Catholic would consent to
either alternative.[83]

One other species of the argument from authority should be considered before we pass on to the examination of the attitude of our authors
towards the place of dialectics in theology. This is the argument from
Eucharistic miracles, closely related to that from universal consent, and
equally despised by Berengar. Eucharistic legends, in which some visible change is reported to have taken place on the altar, were current
in the Middle Ages. In some of them, Christ appeared in the form
of a lovely child, to reward the faith of a believer; in others the Eucharistic species were reported to have changed into a dry cinder, to prevent
the sacrament from being profaned.[84] In the minds of some modern
critics, the existence of these legends has provided further evidence for
the credulity of the Middle Ages, and their use as proofs for the real
presence confirmation of the absurdity of the Catholic doctrine.   But

---

80 Lanf., PL 150: 410 D - 411 C; Guit., PL 149: 1486 D - 1487 A; Alg., PL
180: 760 C; 796 D - 797 B.

81 Lanf., 413 CD: "Ab hac sententia nunquam discessit sanctus Leo in omnibus
conciliis suis. . . . Quae sententia non effugit successorem quoque suum felicis memoriae
papam Victorem. . . . Porro quid de hac re tempore Nicolai gestum sit, breviter supra
reseravi."

82 Guit., 1469 A: "Quocirca hostium machinis, Deo auxiliante, copiose frustratis,
etiam si nil amplius adderemus, sola tibi catholicae fidei sufficere generalis consuetudo
deberet."

83 Lanf., 441 A: "Interroga universos qui Latinae linguae nostrarumve litterarum
notitiam perceperunt. Interroga Graecos, Armenos, seu cujuslibet quoscumque Christianos
homines; uno ore hanc fidem se testantur habere. Porro si universalis Ecclesiae fides
falsa existit, aut nunquam fuit catholica Ecclesia, aut periit. Nihil namque efficacius ad
interitum animarum quam perniciosus error. Sed non fuisse, aut perisse Ecclesiam, catholicus nemo consenserit." Cf. Alg., PL 180:780 A.

84 For a historical summary of these legends, see Roach, W., "Eucharistic Tradition in the *Perlesvaus*," *Zeitschrift für Romanische Philologie*, 59 (1939) 10 - 56.

the theological—as distinguished from the moral—importance of the Eucharistic legends has been vastly exaggerated.[85]   We can see their exact import in the treatise of the opponents of Berengar.

The argument from Eucharistic miracles appears in Lanfranc, Guitmund, and Alger. But in none of these are the legendary marvels brought forth as direct proofs of the truth of the real presence. Our authors say expressly that they do not possess equal weight with the authentic writings.[86]   They are not, in fact, necessary to the proof, since the Catholic doctrine is adequately established without them.[87] Yet they portray graphically a picture of reality, and are therefore "congruous to the Catholic faith."[88]   If they had not expressed truly the content of the universal belief, the stories of them would have been suppressed.

From such a cautious use of this legendary material, it can be clearly seen that Eucharistic legends played but a small part in the medieval theology of the Eucharist. They were not offered directly as proofs of the Catholic doctrine; indeed, the question as to whether they really happened—though our authors would never have denied that they did —did not affect the issue at all. Their value was secondary, auxiliary; they were part of the heritage of the faithful; they illustrated and manifested the faith of the Church.

3. Dialectics

Thus far we have seen in the principles of the Berengarian theology an abundant use of Scripture and tradition, along with an insistence that the sacred writings do not always carry their meaning openly, but

---

85 Roach, *ibid.*, shows that the miracles were never used as theological "proofs," but that their purpose was mainly to edify. With one exception, the miraculous narratives contained in the treatise of Paschasius Radbertus are shown to have been the work of later interpolators: Roach, *ibid.*, p. 28.

86 Lanf., 435 D: "Quae scripturae tametsi illam excelcissimam auctoritatis arcem non obtinet qua donatae sunt quas propheticas seu apostolicas nuncupamus. . . ." Cf. Alg., 779 D.

87 Alg., 779 C: "Quamvis enim ipsius Christi et tot sanctorum testimoniis, et universalis etiam Ecclesiae catholica fide, quae ab initio conversionis suae ita credidit, et ita salvata est, sufficienter adstructum sit, quod vera caro Christi verusque sanguis in mensa Dominica immoletur. . . ."

88 *Ibid.*, ". . . ne quis tamen perversor aliter intelligeret vel exponeret, facta sunt a Deo congrua huic nostrae fidei miracula, . . ." Cf. Lanf., 435 D, Guit., 1480 BC. Guitmund seems to allow greater force to these Eucharistic miracles, and Roach (*loc. cit.*, p. 45) says that they received "a more serious acceptance" after the Berengarian controversy than before — an acceptance due chiefly to the "vigorous defense" of them by Guitmund, as a "competent theologian."

need to be interpreted according to some norm. We have seen the flat rejection of the authority of the Church and of the consent of Catholics as useful norms of interpretation, since according to Berengar the secrets of divine science are but seldom in the possession of the vulgar mob. Consequently, we must now discover what is the norm of interpretation for Berengar, what is the standard against which Revelation is to be tested in order to acquire its inner meaning. And we shall find that he places at the basis of his search for truth the principles and methods of an immature philosophy, the dialectics of the schools. The secrets of the Kingdom of God are to be known, if at all, through the acuteness and penetration of the individual inquiring mind.[89]

---

89 Historians of dogma, Catholic and Protestant, and historians of logic have paid their respects to Berengar's avowed fidelity to tradition, but have been forced to conclude that he accorded it a secondary place:

Cappuyns, "Bérenger de Tours," DHGE 8, 400: Berengar cannot be called rationalist or nominalist. His Eucharistic ideology is of Augustinian origin. It is true he inherited from Fulbert a cultus for dialectics, yet he does not go so far as to contradict in its name Scripture and the Fathers. Yet Cappuyns admits that in the context of the passage he cites in favor of Berengar's regard for tradition appears one of Berengar's strongest statements in favor of the superiority of reason.

Harnack, *o. cit.*, p. 46: Berengar did not revolt against authority, but tried to rescue the *true* tradition of the Church from the embraces of a "bad routine . . . a coarse and superstitious realism." Yet Harnack finds "combined with this interest . . . the pleasure of thinking, and the daring reliance on dialectics, as on 'reason' in general. As theologians, Berengar and his followers were Augustinians, but at the same time, Berengar had an enjoyment in criticism as such, and a confidence in 'science' that were not Augustinian."

Macdonald, *op. cit.*, p. 98: Berengar's devoiton to tradition was sincere, but qualified by his conviction that reason must be applied if the truth underlying the words is to be reached. And this rationalism becomes the basis of the Berengarian system: "In the *De sacra coena* we shall see that this application of the dialectical method, in order to supplement the authority of tradition . . . becomes the foundation of the whole system of Berengar's exegesis." p. 219: "The evangelical principle of the freedom of private judgment was originated in the Middle Ages by Berengar."

Ebersolt, *loc. cit.*, pp. 168-169: "It is true then to say that Berengar did not admit the authority of Scripture except in so far as it was conformed to reason." Thanks to reason we can know the truth in an "immediate manner."

Vernet, "Bérenger de Tours," DTC 2: 728: "Berengar tested the data of faith in the crucible of reason."

Geiselmann, *Die Eucharistielehre der Vorscholastik*, p. 290: "Dialectics becomes . . . the ground principle of his work, . . . the epitome of knowledge."

Grabmann, *Die Geschichte der Scholastischen Methode*, 1, p. 219: "Dialectics is for him the reason, the essence, and the measure of all knowledge."

Prantl, C., *Geschichte der Logik im Abenlande*, vol. II, Leipzig, 1861, p. 72: Berengar "set himself against all authority in the sphere of knowledge, no matter what the authority might be; and in opposition to all tradition . . . recognized as the exclusive measure of truth only his own power of thought." (Note that the historian of logic is bolder in his statements than the historians of dogma. Reuter is similarly bold. See the interesting comment on Reuter in Harnack, *op. cit.*, p. 46, n. 4).

Berengar's theology is almost entirely inspired by his devotion to the supremacy of the rational faculty in man. The faculty of intellect is the glory of man. If man enjoys a position of honor in creation it is because he is endowed with intellect.[90] If Berengar was convinced of anything, it was of the eminence of reason.[91]

In three extremely important pages of the *De sacra coena*—pp. 100-102—Berengar sets down explicitly the basic principles upon which his Eucharistic theology was erected. He says:

> It is clearly the property of a great heart to have recourse to dialectic in all things, because to have recourse to dialectic is to have recourse to reason; and he who refuses this recourse, since it is in the faculty of reason that he is made in the image of God, abandons his own proper glory, and cannot be renewed from day to day in the image of God.[92]

One phrase in this assertion requires special attention, the phrase, "in all things," *per omnia*. It is admitted—indeed the scholastic method is built on this—that one may reason profitably upon the meaning of Scripture and tradition, and upon the divine Mysteries. But we cannot hold that necessarily our reasoning must lead only to conclusions which unaided reason can adequately explain. That is the very formula of rationalism: to subject the divine Mysteries to the limited powers of the finite mind, to deny the revealed character of doctrines which cannot be rationally apprehended. This seems to be the significance of the *per omnia* in the statement of Berengar—not an *obiter dictum* by any means, but an emphatic statement of his conviction, repeated in many ways in the context.

Another important expression of the fundamental theological principle of Berengar is the following:

> You do not hesitate to write of me that I neglect sacred authorities; it shall become clear with the divine assistance that this accusation is a lie and not the truth, since I have placed sacred authorities in my argument wherever the need arose. But to act by reason in the apprehension

---

90 D.s.c., p. 221: "Homo in honore positus, id est, intellectu praeditus."

Ibid., p. 222: "Intellectualitas interioris hominis decus."

91 *Ibid.*, p. 53: ". . . eminentia rationis . . ."

92 *Ibid.*, p. 101: "Maxime plane cordis est, per omnia ad dialecticam confugere. quia confugere ad eam, ad rationem est confugere, quo qui not confugit, cum secundum rationem sit factus ad imaginem Dei, suum honorem reliquit, nec potest renovari de die in diem ad imaginem Dei."

93 Cf. Heurtevent, *op. cit.*, p. 201.

of divine truth is incomparably superior, since [then] the thing is evident — that no one will deny unless madness has blinded him.[94]

The first part of this passage is the one noted by Cappuyns against the application of the term "rationalist" to Berengar.[95] But Berengar's insistence on his regard for authority is followed immediately by a statement of the "incomparable" eminence of reason. The elliptical phrase, "quia in evidenti res est," casts considerable light upon Berengar's theory of religious knowledge. It is a technical phrase with Berengar, appearing several times in the *De sacra coena.*[96] A thing is evident if it can be clearly seen, either properly, by the senses, or, in a transferred sense, by obvious and clear-cut demonstration, so as to exclude the possibility of hidden meaning.[97] The construction which Berengar adopts, "in" with the ablative, "in evidenti," is a rhetorical device to heighten and emphasize the meaning. This construction can be found in Claudius Donatus and in St. Augustine.[98]

If we examine Berengar's meaning it seems we must come to the con-

----

94 D.s.c., p. 100: "Quod relinquere me, inquio ego, sacras auctoritates non dubitas scribere, manifestum fiet divinitate propicia, illud de calumnia scribere te, non de veritate, ubi deducendi sacras auctoritates in medium necessitate inde agendi locus occurrerit, quanquam ratione agere in perceptione veritatis incomparabiliter superius esse, quia in evidenti res est, sine vecordiae coecitate nullus negaverit."

In the English translation which appears in our text, the "res," which is said to be "in evidenti," is taken to refer to the "perceptio veritatis," rather than to the "ratione agere" — the causal "quia" seems to demand this reading. Thus the sense would be: if one acts by reason, he achieves a solution which is "in evidenti."

95 Note 89 *supra.*

96 D.s.c., p. 215: "In evidenti res est, quoque verba convolvas, luce clarius beati Ambrosii sententia eminet" — in connection with Berengar's dialectical distortion of the realist passage from *De myst.*, 9, "Et hoc quod conficimus corpus, ex virgine est."

D.s.c., p. 245: "Dum enim dicis absumi panem . . . contra perspicuae evidentiam veritatis quia in evidenti res est."

97 *Thesaurus linguae latinae* (Teubner), 5: 1036: evidens: apertus, dilucidus, patens; id quod cerni potest; proprie, de iis fere rebus quae visu percipiuntur; translate, id quod manifestum, perspicuum, apertum.

Diefenbach, *Glossarium latino-Germanicum, mediae et infimae aetatis,* Frankfort-on-Main, 1857, p. 212: evidens: merklich (perceptible, perceivable, sensible.)

Ernont and Meillet, *Dictionnaire étymologique de la langue latine,* Paris, 1932, p. 299: evidens: (distinct, visible, in bodily form).

98 T. Claudius Donatus, *Commentum Vergilii Aeneidos,* (ed. Fabricius), Basle, 1561: 1, 50, p. 26, 16: ultionis spes in evidenti constituta; 1, 560, p. 111, 23: aperuit quod fuerit in evidenti; 1, 705, p. 138, 4: in evidenti est . . . quanta . . . fuerit multitudo."

St. Augustine, *In Joannis Evagelium,* 32, 6, PL 35: 1644: "Sed quid est quod ait, *Non enim erat spiritus datus, quia Jesus nondum erat glorificatus?* In evidenti est intellectus. Non enim non erat Spiritus Dei, qui erat apud Deum; sed nondum erat in eis qui crediderant in Jesum" — a passage in which St. Augustine wishes to remove any thought of a hidden or mysterious meaning from the words of Our Lord in St. John 7: 39.

clusion: to follow reason in religious inquiry is better than to follow authority, because the result of rational inquiry is a clear and patent demonstration, while dependence on authority might lead to obscure and hidden meaning—in short, to mystery. It is difficult to take any other meaning out of the text.[99]   If he had used conditional phraseology, his assertion could be understood in a Catholic sense.   There is no reason why one should follow authority *if* the matter is evident.[100] But he has expressed himself in the most general terms: reason is incomparably superior to authority *because* the truth then becomes evident.   This is a statement of rationalism; given wider extension than Berengar thought to give it, it would lead to the rejection of all mystery in religion and thus to skepticism.

Berengar is always emphatic upon the superiority of reason over authority.   A man of spirit would prefer to perish, if he had the option, rather than to yield to authority.[101]   The argument from authority is a poor substitute for that from reason, and the same superiority exists in the relation between reason and faith.[102]

Taking into account, then, the superiority of rational inquiry over traditional teaching as clearly held by Berengar, we may expect to find in his Eucharistic theology a rationalism far more extreme than that of any Catholic author.   To cite Harnack, "Here, for the first time, the categories 'subiectum', 'quod in subiecto', 'de subiecto', the distinction of 'esse' from 'secundum quod esse', in short the dialectical manipulations of the notion of substance (according to Porphyry, Boethius, etc.) were

---

99 Here there is a close similarity to the passage noted above at p. 46, n. 41, where Berengar says it is difficult or even impossible for him to interpret St. Ambrose *ad normam . . . manifestorum*. It seems that "manifestorum" would have the same meaning as "in evidenti;" and Berengar's meaning would be: It is difficult to interpret St. Ambrose according to a norm of manifest meaning — in other words, so as to exclude all mystery. Cf. Ebersolt, *loc. cit.*, pp. 168-9. "This faculty of reason is necessary in his eyes to discover the true meaning of Scripture; thanks to it we can know the truth *in an immediate manner.*"

100 S. Th., 2-2, q. 1, aa. 4 & 5.

101 D.s.c. 102: "Circa dialecticam, quantum oportet, satagenti de videndo luce clarius Deo et anima spondere in eodem libro minime dubitavit Augustinus, nec sequendus in eo es ulli cordato homini, ut malit auctoritatibus circa aliqua credere, quam ratione. si optio sibi datur, perire."

102 *Ibid.*, p. 215: "Cede auctoritati, si ad rationem non sufficis." p. 214: "Si non sufficis quod dico, ratione comprehendere." p. 230: ". . . oportet to hoc fide tenere, si ratiocinari non sufficis."

applied to a dogma in the west."[103] Berengar was far from the first to apply dialectics to dogma, but it is true, as Geiselmann has pointed out, that this dialectical treatment, which had been considered by earlier writers as an aid and handmaid to divine science, became in Berengar the foundation stone of his work.[104]   And since the philosophy upon which he based his thought was immature and undeveloped, it led him into philosophical error which was the radical cause of his Eucharistic heresy.   In connection with the Mystery of Faith, it was fatal for Berengar "to laugh at faith, to will to comprehend everything through reason."[105]

When we study the attitude toward dialectics of Berengar's opponents, we have the impression that the farther removed the writer from the heresiarch himself, the less self-conscious he was upon this problem. Guitmund, for example, uses dialectical arguments constantly, matter-of-factly, without apology or justification. His language is always that of the dialecticians of the schools, and in some respects his terminology is an improvement on that of the arch-dialectician Berengar, substituting, for example, the term "accidens" for the more cumbrous "quod in subiecto est" of Berengar.[106] Guitmund claims that he will establish the truth of his position by means of the strongest possible demonstration, the "ratio necessaria;" but he saves himself from rationalism by saying he will prove by "necessary reason" only the *fact* that God has done what He willed to do, which was to effect a substantial change; but *how* He has done it remains an impenetrable mystery.[107] Alger of Liége, no less than Guitmund, pursues his theological method without any particular attempt to explain it: authority and reason—an elaborate collection of patristic texts, and a free use of dialectic to explain them.

Only Lanfranc, who met the adversary face to face, who recognized with clearest penetration the fundamental error of the heresiarch, is self-conscious upon the question of method, and expresses himself as ex-

---

103 *Op. cit.*, p. 46. Cf. Lanfranc's comment, PL 150: 418 D: "Quod vero dialectica verba, affirmationem, praedicatum, subjectum, caeteraque in hunc modum tractatui tantae rei laboras inserere, propter nihil aliud videris id facere nisi ut hac occasione peritum te disputandi imperitis valeas suadere."

104 *Op. cit.*, p. 290.

105 Lanf. 427 B: ". . . fidem arridere, rationibus omnia velle comprehendere."

106 Guit., PL 149: 1450 B, etc.

107 *Ibid.*, 1441 C: "Quod eum voluisse Deum ipso adjuvante opportuno loco monstraverimus, sive possit intellegi quomodo fiat, sive non possit, obtinebimus tamen necessaria ratione quoniam fecit. Non enim satis argumento est, si nostrae indirimitatis caecitas id nunquam in hac vita capere valeat, quominus debeas credere, si manifestae rationis necessitas, rem ita ut diximus, probavit esse."

tremely reluctant to undertake a dialectical defense of the Catholic doctrine. Some historians of dogma have seen in this reluctance of Lanfranc to use rational arguments the weakness of his work.[108] It is
rather difficult to expain, in view of Lanfranc's reputation as a dialectician. He had received an excellent education in liberal arts and in
law, and was known as an accomplished advocate. Sigebert of Gembloux signalizes in Lanfranc's commentaries on St. Paul his use of the
dialectical method;[109] though Lanfranc, in the same connection, claimed that he wished to follow the teaching of the Holy Spirit, as St. Paul
did, rather than the rules of liberal arts.[110]

Lanfranc has set down his viewpoint on the question of the dialectical method in an interesting passage of his treatise. He says that he
would far prefer the entire controversy to be carried on through the
appeal to sacred authorities, rather than through dialectical arguments;
and he calls God and his conscience to witness that this is the truth.[111]
He makes the rather odd assertion that even in matters where a dialectical procedure would be both legitimate and suitable, he should prefer
to "conceal the art," and try to achieve the end without using the means,
lest he give the impression of confiding more in reason than in authority.[112] Yet he is willing to acknowledge that the utility of dialectics
even in questions of faith has the high authority of St. Augustine in its
favor; he feels that he can give Berengar as much as he takes from him;
and therefore he will follow him onto that ground with reluctance,

---

108 E. Amann and A. Gaudel, "Lanfranc," DTC 8: 2658: 'It is regrettable that
by reaction against the exaggerated confidence of Berengar in dialectics, the abbot of
St. Stephen uses it so scantily himself to explain, defend and interpret his faith: before
the 'how' of the mystery and the miracle, he is satisfied with appealing to another miracle, taking an attitude of humble reserve, and confessing the uselessness of speculation.
In this he is of his time, and Hugh of St. Victor, a century later, will use the same
language (PL 176: 462). The philosophy which will permit St. Thomas to propose a
rational explanation of the Eucharist dogma is not yet known."

109 Sigebert, *Liber de scriptoribus ecclesiasticis*, PL 160: 582: "Lanfrancus dialecticus et Cantuarensis archiepiscopus Paulum apostolum exposuit, et ubicumque opportuni-
tas locorum occurit, secundum leges dialecticae proponit, assumit, concludit."

110 Lanfranc, *In D. Pauli Epistolas commentarium*, PL 150: 163 B: "Unde procul dubio est non eum regulas artium saecularium in scribendo vel loquendo cogitasse,
sed per doctrinam Spiritus Sancti . . . talia et taliter dixisse, quae per singula exponerem. . . ."

111 Lanf., 416 D: "Et quidem de mysterio fidei auditurus ac responsurus quae ad
rem debeant pertinere, mallem audiere ac respondere sacras auctoritates quam dialecticas
rationes."
Ibid., 417 A: "Sed testis mihi est Deus, et conscientia mea. . . ."

112 *Ibid.*, "Etsi quando materia disputandi talis est up (per) hujus artis regulas
valeat enucleatius explicari, in quantum possum, per aequipollentias propositionum tego
artem, ne videar magis arte quam veritate sanctorumque Patrum auctoritate confidere."

knowing as he does that some will lay his dialectical arguments to pride rather than to real necessity.[113]

With such a cautious preamble, we are not surprised to see in Lanfranc many expressions of the uselessness of attempting to penetrate deeply into the Mystery of the Eucharist;[114] and a general treatment which, though quite useful in preparing the ground, left much room for development in those writers who would follow.[115]

Nevertheless, in the one pitched battle which he had with Berengar on a point of purely formal dialectics, Lanfranc clearly came out on top. In the lost *opusculum* against which Lanfranc's treatise was written, Berengar claimed to find in the Humbertian formula of 1059 an open contradiction according to the laws of dialectical reasoning. The Humbertian formula was, in part:

> Panis et vinum, quae ponuntur in altari, post consecrationem [solummodo] sunt verum Christi corpus et sanguis.[116]

Berengar's point was that where the two terms of an affirmative proposition are united by a copula of identity, the subject must be contained in the predicate, or the whole proposition will break down. That is to say, when Humbert affirmed that the bread and wine of the altar are the Body and Blood of Christ, he also affirms by that very statement that the bread and wine remain. However, when the Archdeacon expressed his argument in form, he took as his major a particular negation, rather than a universal: *"Not every* proposition can stand if part breaks down;"* rather than, *"No* proposition can stand if part breaks down."* So that Berengar's argument was, in form:

> MAJOR: Not every proposition can stand if part breaks down.
> MINOR: But the proposition, "The bread and wine of the altar are [only] the Body and Blood of Christ," is an affirmation consisting of subject and predicate.
> CONCLUSION: Therefore, even though the Burgundian [Humbert] attempted to deny that the bread and wine remain, yet by his affirmation he simply confirms that they do remain.[117]

Lanfranc answered this formal argument by pointing out its fatal defect

---

113 *Ibid.*

114 *Ibid.*, 421, 427 etc.

115 E. Amann and A. Gaudel, *loc. cit.*, col. 2658: "Lanfranc is satisfied to expose clearly the object of faith. As for seeking out the nature of the substantial conversion of the bread and wine, how it is done, he believes that a useless task: the believer ought not to occupy himself with scrutinizing such a mystery."

116 This is Berengar's phrasing, cited from his *opusculum* by Lanfranc, 418 C. The word *solummodo* has been placed in brackets, because it is Berengar's word, not Humbert's; it did not appear in formula of 1059, and Lanfranc will call this to Berengar's attention repeatedly in developing his theory of the Eucharist as a Sacrament.

117 Lanf., 416 D: 418 C.

in form: it is impossible to conclude anything from two particular premises. If Berengar is to conclude anything from his argument, he must make his major premise a universal negation.[118] It must be confessed that the whole discussion was rather trivial. Berengar's argument, even apart from its defect of form, contained a patent sophism. Humbert's formula might not have been happily chosen, leaving out as it did any direct reference to a change; but its meaning was clear, and Berengar's argument failed to take account of the words of consecration, a practical proposition, by which the real presence of Christ's Body and Blood is brought about. No Catholic would hold that Humbert's proposition, "The bread and wine of the altar are the Body and Blood of Christ," is a simply speculative proposition expressing identity. And Lanfranc's reply equally overlooks the main weakness of the argument and attacks it for its defect of form. In fact, the argument would not have been stronger even if it had been properly laid. But the discussion is interesting in the light that it casts upon the love of our authors for matching wits in dialectics, and it contains a key point in Berengar's attack on the doctrine of a substantial change. At any rate, in the *De sacra coena* the Archdeacon admits that he had laid the argument improperly, and sets about with great zeal to recast it, though he criticizes Lanfranc for attacking the argument upon the form rather than the substance.[119]

---

118 *Ibid.*, 417 D: "Adhuc alio argumento probare contendis panem vinumque post consecrationem in principalibus permanere essentiis, dicens, 'Non enim constare poterit affirmatio omnis, parte subruta.' Ad cujus rei probationem non oportuit inferri particularem negationem, qua de praesenti quaestione nihil colligitur, sed universalem potius, per quam enuntiatur, nulla affirmatio constare poterit parte subruta. Age, enim particularis sit negatio tua . . . rursus assumptio tua: Panis et vinum altaris solummodo sunt sacramentum, vel panis et vinum altaris solummodo sunt verum Christi corpus et sanguis utrumque affrmatio est. His duabus particularibus praecedentibus, poterisne regulariter concludere, parte subruta, ea non posse constare? Absit! In nulla quippe syllogismorum figura, praecedentibus duabus particularibus, consequenter infertur conclusio ulla. Male igitur eam collocasti."

119 D.s.c., p. 110: ". . . quod male syllogismum collocaverim, moram facis, circa rem ipsam nec transeunter agas."

Macdonald, *op. cit.*, pp. 292-3, discusses the point in the light of the various opinions of nineteenth century historians of logic. In a note on p. 293, he cites De Ghellinck, "Dialectique et dogme au Xe - XIIe siècle," p. 78, as the source for a statement that De Ghellinck thinks this criticism the best part of Lanfranc's treatise, which is otherwise inferior to that of Alger. But it is difficult to draw that precise meaning from De Ghellinck's comment in that place.

The attitude of R. L. Poole, in *Illustrations of Medieval Thought and Learning* has been discussed before (p. 20, n. 26). It is to be expected that Poole would deny any merit to Lanfranc as a dialectician in comparison with Berengar. He writes (p. 90): "Archbishop Lanfranc, a learned man and a good lawyer, was greatest in the practical affairs of the state: in dialectical warfare he showed but poorly. He vanquished Berengar by transparent sophisms. Logic in his hands was an imperfect instrument which he had not fully learned to use."

CHAPTER IV

THE CONTROVERSY CONCERNING THE SUBSTANTIAL CONVERSION

1. *The Berengarian Critique*

In its general structure, the Eurcharistic theology of Berengar of
Tours presents a double aspect, consisting negatively in a dialectical attack on the doctrine of the substantial conversion, which he thought
contradictory and absurd; and positively, in an attempt to build up a
theology of the Eucharist as sacrament, mere sign and symbol. It is
true that the two aspects are not entirely distinct: his theory of the
Eucharist as sacrament provided him with what he considered one of
his strongest arguments against a substantial conversion, since it is of
the essence of a sacrament that it point to some reality which is not contained within itself. The logical mind of Berengar balked at the idea
that the Eucharist be at one and the same time the Body of Christ and
the sacrament of the Body of Christ. The two aspects are, however,
clearly recognizeable in his teaching, and they will be taken up re-
spectively in this and the following chapter. It should perhaps be remarked also that it is wholly fair to Berengar to discuss his system
almost exclusively from the viewpoint of his dialectics, with little attention to his scriptural and patristic documentation. His opinion of the
relative importance of reason and authority has been sufficiently determined. One thing is certainly true of Berengar, whatever its final import will be: he built on reason, not on faith.

The negative aspect of his thought, the criticism of the theory of
substantial change, may itself be subdivided into a threefold argumentation: first, an argument of the metaphysical order, based upon his
concept of being; second, an argument drawn from a dialectical analysis
of the concept of change; and third, a dialectical attack upon the language of the Humbertian formula of 1059. The three arguments are
closely related, dovetailing at many points; but the first is basic and
fundamental, the philosophical position upon which Berengar erected
his system. The section of this chapter, then, which concerns the teaching of Berengar, will consist in an analysis of his three principal arguments against the doctrine of a substantial conversion.

It has already been pointed out that dialectics, although it was the
principal element, did not however constitute the totaliy of pre-scholast-

ic philosophy. It is true that the pre-scholastic philosophers, following Boethius, thought of logic as concerned mainly with words, not things; but since words are the signs of reality, they could not resist speculating upon the nature of the reality that lay behind the words. Grabmann has remarked that all the important elements of a whole philosophy are to be found in germ in Boethius. Consequently it is not at all surprising that Berengar, attempting to analyze rationally the Eucharist, a concrete object which appears to the senses as a fragment of bread and a cup of wine, should have permitted himself to speculate about the meaning of concrete being as such. In the *De sacra coena,* therefore, whether he was fully aware of it or not,[1] Berengar introduced into the formulas of the dialectical procedure a metaphysical principle.

The Berengarian concept of being appears in certain important passages of the *De sacra coena* which require a careful analysis:

(p. 211:) "Omne compactum ex materia et forma, aliud est in eo quod est, aliud in eo quod aliquid est; nec posse aliquid esse si contigerit ipsum non esse, id est, quod secundum subiectum non sit, minime secundum accidens esse."

Everything composed of matter and form, is one thing in that it is, another in that it is something. And it cannot be something if it no longer exists; that is, whatever does not exist as a subject cannot exist as an accident.

(p. 92) "Constat autem omne, quod constet ex materia et forma, vel quarumcumque proprietatum confluentia, ipsum quod est maxime debere formae, et si esse per corruptionem subiecti desierit, maxime illud quoque amissioni formae necessario imputari."

Everything which is composed of matter and form, or of the coming together of the properties of a thing, owes its [determined] existence mainly to the form; and if it ceases to exist through a destruction of the subject, this also is due mainly to the loss of form.[2]

The inherent difficulty of these two passages, dealing as they do with the primal constituents of being, is greatly increased by Berengar's intricate style and terminology; but it is possible and necessary to extricate the exact meaning of Berengar.

For Berengar, then, the corporeal object is composed of matter and form: "omne compactum ex materia et forma"—these are the two principles of being. Matter is the principle of existence of a thing as

---

1 Geiselmann, *op. cit.,* p. 360: "wenn auch unbewusst."

2 Obviously the meaning here is not that everything is two things, one that is, and one that is something. The attempt has been made to translate the two passages literally, to avoid the introduction of new terminology by way of paraphrase. What is concerned is a twofold principle of being. Cf. D.s.c., pp. 70, 92.

yet undetermined: "aliud est in eo quod est;" while form is the principle of specification, by which a *thing* becomes a determined *something*: "aliud in eo quod aliquid est." Thus "materia" indicates merely *that-a-thing-is*, while it is the task of the correlative principle, "forma," to determine *what-a-thing-is*.[3] The form of bread, for example, is that principle by which bread is, not a stone, not flesh, but bread.[4] Matter gives to an object existence, while form gives to it specific and determined existence.[5]

Thus, in the metaphysics of Berengar, the essential principles of corporeal substance are matter and form. Berengar does not use the abstract term, "substance;" but his concrete term, "subiectum," is nothing other than substance individualized and existing in a determined thing. Matter and form must come togther if the subject is to exist. And the precise function of the form is to determine the specific character of the subject, to determine what-it-is.

But it is of capital importance to observe that in his discussion of "forma" Berengar fails to distinguish between *substantial* form and those additional and non-essential determinations which philosophy calls *accidental* forms. For Berengar, the form includes all of the ordinary properties of the corporeal object: "vel quarumcumque proprietatum confluentia." The form gives shape to the object, size, color, all of those properties by which we recognize an object for what it is and distinguish it from others. Accidental forms enter into the essential composition of the "subiectum," and it is therefore unthinkable that the subject itself should pass away, and that the accidents should remain: "quod secundum subiectum non sit, minime secundum accidens esse." [6] Berengar's "subiectum," then, is a determined corporeal substance composed of matter and form as essential principles. But Berengar's "forma" includes accidental forms as well as substantial form. And

---

3 Cf. Geiselmann, *op. cit.*, p. 338: "Materia ist Prinzip des Seins (esse), forma des Soseins (aliquid esse).

4 D.s.c., p. 93.

5 Cf. the different explanation of Macdonald, *op. cit.*, p. 317: "According to Berengar, everything has two properties. It is one thing in that which it is. It is another thing in the sense in which anything is. . . . His meaning is that everything is one thing in its special identity, and another thing so far as it shares its "materia" or substance with everything else — so far as it is universal." But Macdonald's introduction of the universal idea into Berengar's "esse aliquid" seems unsatisfactory. Berengar is speaking only of the essential principles which constitute the being of a determined object.

6 It is significant here that Berengar uses the term "accidens," while overlooking its obvious philosophical denotation: that is, a *non-essential* principle of determination.

from this we must conclude that Berengar wholly failed to discern the real distinction between substance and accident.

This metaphysical error is the explanation of Berengar's thoroughly sensist concept of being. In the Aristotelian system which was to prevail in scholastic philosophy, the senses do not come into direct and immediate contact with substance considered precisely as substance. The senses perceive only the accidental, the changing and the moving; while the inner reality of things, the substance itself, is the pure object of the intellect, since only the intellect can apprehend being-as such, *sub ratione entis*. It is true that sense perception provides normally the only trustworthy basis upon which a judgment as to the substance may be founded, and in this sense, we know substance through the accidents. But nevertheless, the substance, the object of intellect, remains really distinct from the accident, the object of sense; and when this concept of being is applied to the Eucharist, it effectually precludes the charge of intellectual absurdity.[7]

But the thought of Berengar is far removed from this. For Berengar, it is not true to say that the proper object of sight is a "colored object," and that the intellectual faculty must enter in by a process of abstraction, however instantaneous that may be, to discover its inward essence. Rather, the eye pierces to the essence itself: the corporeal object is sensible by its essence; it is all that the senses tell us it is, and it is nothing but that. If anyone sees the color of marble, he does not see merely the color, but the marble itself, since the reason why he is

---

7 The difference between the Berengarian and the scholastic concept of being is brought out in the following table:

Berengarian	Scholastic
ESSENTIAL PRINCIPLES OF BEING	
Constituting "Substance"	
MATTER: principle of undetermined existence: "Ipsum Esse."	MATTER: undetermined principle which receives the substantial form.
FORM: principle of determination: "Aliquid Esse." Includes both substantial and accidental forms — in fact, no distinction is made between them.	FORM: the principle of determination which gives specific character to matter.
NON-ESSENTIAL PRINCIPLES OF BEING	
NONE	ACCIDENTS: additional determinations of substance which are really distinct from substance. Their actual separation from substance in the Eucharist, therefore, does not involve a contradiction.

able to see the color is that he sees the marble, the subject.[8]   If your face is colored black, I cannot see the color unless I also see your face.[9] It is altogether clear that in no way can color be seen, unless the colored object is also seen.[10]

In his application to the Eucharist of this concept of being, Berengar was of course compelled to hold as metaphysically absurd Lanfranc's doctrine of total change of "inner essence," while the "visible appearances" remain.[11]   The bread cannot cease to be bread and yet retain, as Lanfranc says, "certain qualities" of bread, for these qualities pertain to the essential form of bread, and if the qualities are present, the bread is present too.[12]   Lanfranc is so stupid as to assert that the flesh of Christ is sensibly on the altar, that the flesh is colored, that the color is seen—and yet that the flesh itself remains invisible.[13]   But in the estimation of Berengar his own logic is inexorable.   If anything is sensibly on the altar it must be seen; and if anything is seen, it cannot be other than its appearances proclaim it to be.[14]   Berengar of course erred in attributing to the Catholics the belief that after the Consecration the accidents of bread inhere in Christ's Body as their subject;[15]

---

8 D.s.c., p. 182: "Quis videns colorem marmoris . . . vel quodcumque in subiecto illo sit marmore, contendat vecordissimus, se colorem illum et non marmor videre, cum causa videndi coloris cuiuscunque, quod in subiecto est, subiecti ipsius visio sit?"

9 *Ibid.*, p. 127: ". . . si supervestiatur facies tua colore Aethiopis, necesse est faciem tuam videri, si colorem illum constituerit videri."

10 D.s.c., p. 171: "Et apud eruditos enim constat, et eis, qui vecordes non sint, omnino est perceptibile, nulla ratione colorem videri, nisi contingat etiam coloratum videri."

Harnack, *op. cit.*, p. 49, n. 4, has an interesting note on Berengar's sensist metaphysics: "Here Berengar emphasized the correct logical reflection, 'quod in subiecto erat superesse quacunque ratione non potest corrupto subiecto,' (D.s.c., p. 93) i.e. when the substance is destroyed, the essential attributes (taste, color, form) cannot remain behind; or p. 59: 'non potest res ulla aliquid esse, si desinat ipsum esse.' Even Protestant historians will take no account of such reasons."

11 Berengar's statement of Lanfranc's doctrine appears in D.s.c., p. 92: "Posse aliquid absumi per corruptionem subiecti, cuius tamen proprietates minime absumantur, revera supersint." Cf. p. 93.

12 D.s.c., p. 92: "Quod autem scribis: cuius nonnullas retinet qualitates . . . multum te errare manifestas."

D.s.c., p. 93: "Contra nunquam quilibet panis esse per corruptionem subiecti desinet, nisi id, per quod non lapis, non caro, sed panis, erat, forte amiserit."

13 *Ibid.*, p. 182: "Quid porro vecordius dici potuit, quam quod tu dicis, carnem esse sensualiter in altari, et eam carnem colorem habere, eumque colorem, qui in subiecto sit carne, videri oculis corporis, ut caro ipsa maneat invisibilis?"

14 *Ibid.*, p. 127: Dicebas enim portiunculam illam carnis Christi panis esse colore adopertam, quod dicens, asserere eam invisibilem non poteras."

15 D.s.c., p. 182: ". . . et eam carnem colorem habere, eumque colorem, qui in subiecto sit carne. . . ."

but this is a finer point of Catholic doctrine which he could not well have learned from Lanfranc's treatise. Lanfranc had not handled it explicitly; the point awaited clarification from Alger of Liége.

Berengar's second argument against the doctrine of substantial conversion was drawn from his analysis of the concept of change as it was conceived in the dialectical tradition. According to the pseudo-Augustinian *Categoriae decem,*[16] the process of "movement,"[17] or substitution, by which one concrete object begins to exist in place of another, is accomplished in one of three ways: the passage from non-being to being: "generatio subiecti," from being to non-being: "corruptio subiecti," or from being to being: "subiectum in subiectum."[18] Only the last of these may properly be called "change," since it alone involves two terms really existing. The author of the *Categoriae decem* distinguishes "immutation," which is the process of substitution generally considered, from "commutation," or change, and makes the latter a species of the former.[19]

When Berengar studied Lanfranc's doctrine in the light of these distinctions, he concluded that the theory of a substantial change of bread and wine did not involve true change at all, but a double process, a substitution of one subject in place of another. The bread ceases to exist by a destruction of the subject; the Body of Christ begins to exist by a generation of the subject.[20] According to Lanfranc, the effect of consecration is that the elements, the bread and wine, cease to exist in their own proper nature.[21] The elements are therefore annihilated as substantial principles,[22] but continue to exist as accidents.[23] And to replace them the Body and Blood of Christ enter in their own proper being.[24] But such a process must truly involve a new beginning of the Body of Christ, a true *generatio subjecti,* an effect which results from

---

16 [St. Augustine], *Categoriae decem,* PL 32: 1419-1440.

17 *Ibid.,* col. 1439: "De motu."

18 *Ibid.,* "Omnis immutatio . . . fit tribus modis: aut ex non subiecto in subiectum; . . . aut ex subiecto in non subiectum; . . . aut ex subiecto in subiectum, ut est motus."

19 *Ibid.,* col. 1440: "Namque immutatio genus est, commutatio species subiecta motui, quam immutationis speciem diximus."

20 D.s.c., p. 90: ". . . fit de pane per generationem subiecti sui et corruptionem subiecti ipsius panis. . . .

21 *Ibid.,* p. 122: "secundum proprietatem naturae."

22 *Ibid.,* p. 69: "quasi consecratio aliqua illud, quod consecretur, per corruptionem subiecti absumat."

23 *Ibid.,* p. 220: "minime secundum subiectum, secundum materialem proprietatem, sed secundum accidens."

24 *Ibid.:* "cruorem secundum materialem proprietatem."

the destruction of the bread, as a cause.[25] On no point is Berengar more insistent than that the realist doctrine involves an innovation on the part of Christ's Body and Blood, a beginning of existence for Christ Himself[26]—and such a thing, of course, is impossible.

Along with his view of a double process of destruction and generation went Berengar's grossly materialistic conception of the theory of his opponents. He attributed gratuitously to Paschasius and Lanfranc the opinion that after the Consecration, the Body of Christ begins to exist on the altar, not in its entirety, but in "little pieces:"

> According to the error of the mob, and of the monk, Paschasius, there is nothing in the altar after the Consecration but a little portion of Flesh and Blood.[27]

It is true that at rare intervals he seems to fall away from this position,[28] but generally he alludes to the orthodox view in the crudest terms,[29] and the *portiuncula carnis et sanguinis* appears endlessly repeated throughout his treatise.[30]

But such a view as he understood it—that the bread and wine should be annihilated, that the Body of Christ, or a portion of it, should begin to exist sensibly on the altar, and yet itself remain unseen—was monstrous to Berengar, and entangled in contradition. In the first place it seemed to him incompatible with divine Providence that God should annihilate an existing thing.[31] And even if bread could be destroyed it was even more absurd that the Body of Christ should have a new beginning on the altar. The thought of a beginning of Christ's Body is incompatible with the Christian religion.[32] Christ has been in heaven for a thousand years, seated at the right hand of His Father in glorious immortality. He will leave the heavenly throne only for the

---

25 *Ibid.*, p. 94: "causa fuerunt generationi."

26 *Ibid.*, p. 245: "quia in evidenti res est, Christi corpus . . . minime nunc posse incipere. . . ."

Ibid.: "tu desipis nunc primum esse incipere."

Ibid., p. 90: "nec potest usquequaque nunc incipere esse."

Cf. pp. 91, 200, 203, 244, 252, etc.

27 *Ibid.*, p. 174: "Secundum errorem vulgi atque Paschasii monachi, nichil esse in altari post consecrationem nisi portiunculam carnis et sanguinis."

28 D.s.c., p. 245: "Christi corpus, tam pro toto, quam pro parte."

29 *Ibid.*, p .281: "in ipsam Christi corporis massam."

30 *Ibid.*, pp. 45, 81, 84, 109, 114, 119, 127, 130, 140, 168, 189, 194, 197, 203, 242.

31 *Ibid.*, p. 246.

32 *Ibid.*, p. 91, 96 ff.

last judgment. Before the end of time, therefore, a presence of Christ's Body on earth is impossible.[33]

Moreover, it is the view of Lanfranc, according to Berengar, that a little portion of Christ's flesh is on the altar, and that this little portion is broken by the hands of the priest and torn by the teeth of the faithful. But such a view would destroy the impassibility of the Risen Body of the Saviour. The Flesh of Christ is imperishable; it is no longer subject to suffering.[34] Portions of His Body cannot be on the altar unless His Body is cut up in heaven and the pieces placed on the altar.[35] But the Body of Christ cannot be cut up into sections, because it is incorruptible.

And further, continues Berengar, even in the supposition that the Body of Christ in the Eucharist is not cut up into sections, but is whole and entire in one Host, then it could not at the same time be present in other Hosts.[36] For Berengar, every corporeal object is essentially subject to the laws of space, and the heavenly Body of Christ is no exception. If the Body of Christ were actually present on the altar, there would be in existence at the same time a million bodies of Christ.[37] Lanfranc calls the Eucharistic Flesh invisible, but the glorious Body of Christ, though incorruptible, is visible and palpable, entirely subject to corporality.[38] It is impossible that the Body should be sensibly present on the altar; and if it were sensibly present, it would have to be sensibly seen.[39]

There is another process by which one object may begin to exist in

33 *Ibid.*, pp. 90-91: "Non ergo caro Christi, quae per mille iam annos constat immortalitate, nec potest usquequaque nunc incipere esse, fit de pane per generationem subiecti sui et corruptionem subiecti ipsium panis, quia caro illa nec absumi potest, quia immortalis et incorruptibilis est, ut destructa et restituta, iterum esse incipiat."
Cf. pp. 94 ff., 148 f., 203, 244.

34 *Ibid.*, p. 34: "incorruptibile." Cf. p. 206; p. 45; "impassibilitatem evangelizat Paulus."

35 *Ibid.*, p. 200: "Portiunculam Christi in altari adesse, fieri non potest, nisi in coelo corpus Christi desecetur et desecta de eo particula ad altare submittatur."
Cf. pp. 203, 244.

36 *Ibid.*, p. 158: "nec ultra per partes desecari contingat;" p. 145: "insecabile quia incorruptibile."

37 *Ibid.*, p. 198.

38 *Ibid.*, p. 247: "minimeque portiunculam ipsam videri, videri tamen colorem, qui sit in subiecto;" p. 195: "visibile et palpabile." Cf. pp. 199, 200, 247.

39 *Ibid.*, p. 158: "tu tamen inconcessibilis hoc fecisti, qui negare persistis, carnem Christi et sanguinem, quae adesse post consecrationem in sacrificio tu confingis sensualiter, videri oculis corporis in altari."
Cf. pp. 149, 198 ff., 244, etc.

place of another, not through a double process of annihilation and substitution, but through a change of form. Gold can become a ring, brass a dish, marble can be shaped into a pear, and wood into a table. In each of these cases, the original material remains, and has simply received a new form through the workmanship of a divine or human artificer.[40] But such a process is exactly the opposite of the change which Lanfranc alleges to have taken place in the Eucharist, where the material is said to have changed, while the form remains. And the original objection of Berengar applies again: "non potest res aliquid esse, si desinat ipsum esse."[41] Moreover, to assert that Christ's Body could take up new qualities, the form of bread, for example, would suppose some perfectibility in Him, some lack which new forms could supply.[42] But such a thought is degrading to Christ.

In sum, Berengar's critique of realism based upon the dialectical analysis of the concept of change led him to the conclusion that the orthodox opinion was contradictory at every point. That bread and wine should be destroyed and replaced by Christ's Body beginning to exist upon the altar is contradictory to the immortality of Christ in glory for a thousand years. That little pieces of His Body should be really present on the altar would destroy His impassibility and incorruptibility. On the other hand, a view that His Body is in the Eucharist whole and entire would annul the unity of the Body, since a corporeal object, subject to the laws of space, can exist in only one place at a time. Again, the theory that Christ's Body is invisible on the altar, though clothed with the accidents of bread, would oppose the corporality of Christ's glorified Body, and would lead to the further absurdity that the essential properties of an object may remain even though the object itself has ceased to exist. And finally, it will be useless for his opponents to claim that there is involved here a simple change *a subiecto in subiectum,* since such a change requires necessarily that its final term be something which did not exist before the change took place, and is brought into existence through a change of form. But in this alleged Eucharistic change, the term, the Body of Christ, is already in existence, while no

---

40 D.s.c., p. 79: "iure materiae nomine appelantur, quod facta sunt de materia, quia non amisit ipsa materia formam suam, ut per corruptionem subiecti transiret in aliud, sed idem subiectum propter eam, quam habebat, aliam nutu divino aut artificis studio formam accepit."

41 *Ibid.,* p. 59.

42 *Ibid.,* p. 95: "qui Christi corpus asserit adhuc esse corruptioni vel generationi obnoxium, vel quarumcumque qualitatum vel collineationum, quas prius non habuerit, susceptivum. . . ."

change of form takes place. This is a pattern of absurdity to Berengar, unworthy of God, and incomprehensible to reason.

Berengar's third major point in his argument against the substantial conversion consisted in an attack on the phrasing of the formula to which he had been compelled to give assent at Rome in 1059. This formula is of primary importance in the history of the controversy.[43] We have already seen how Lanfranc formally demolished Berengar's poorly phrased argument in the earlier treatise; and we shall see the term *solummodo* of the formula entering into the dispute concerning the nature of the sacrament. But we are interested here in its use by Berengar as an argument against the substantial conversion.

The formula of 1059 was the work of Cardinal Humbert. In its positive part, this formula carried the phrase,

> The bread and wine which are placed on the altar, after the Consecration, are not only a sacrament, but also the true Body and Blood of Our Lord, Jesus Christ.[44]

In the earlier *opusculum*, Berengar attempted to turn this expression against Humbert, saying that "the enemy of truth willy-nilly asserts the truth."[45] Humbert, the enemy of truth, intended to deny that the bread and wine remain; but by placing bread and wine as subject of an affirmative proposition he merely asserted that they do remain. Thus Humbert, against his will, testified to the truth, namely that the bread and wine remain.

In the *De sacra coena*, Berengar rectified the error of form which

---

43 Lanf., PL 150: 410D—411 A: "Ego Berengarius, indignus diaconus Ecclesiae Sancti Mauricii Andegavensis, cognoscens veram catholicam et apostolicam fidem, anathematizo omnem haeresim, praecipue eam de qua hactenus infamatus sum, quae astruere conatur panem et vinum quae in altari ponuntur, post consecrationem solummodo sacramentum, et non verum corpus et sanguinem Domini nostri Jesu Christi esse, nec posse sensualiter in solo sacramento manibus sacerdotum tractari, vel frangi, aut fidelium dentibus atteri. Consentio autem sanctae Romanae et apostolicae sedi, et ore et corde profiteor de sacramentis Dominicae mensae eam fidem tenere quam dominus et venerabilis papa Nicolaus, et haec sancta synodus auctoritate evangelica et apostolica tenendam tradidit, mihique firmavit; scilicet panem et vinum quae in altari ponuntur, post consecrationem non solum sacramentum, sed etiam verum corpus et sanguinem Domini nostri Jesu Christi esse, et sensualiter non solum sacramento, sed in veritate manibus sacerdotum tractari, frangi, et fidelium dentibus atteri, jurans per sanctam et homoousion Trinitatem, et per haec sacrosancta Christi Evangelia. Eos vero qui contra hanc fidem venerint, cum dogmatibus et sectatoribus suis aeterno anathemate dignos esse pronuntio. Quod si ego ipse aliquando aliquid contra haec sentire aut praedicare praesumpsero, subjaceam canonum severitati. Lecto et perlecto sponte subscripsi."

44 Lanf., PL 150: 411 A.

45 *Ibid.*, 413 B: "Quia veritatis inimicus, velit nolit, veritatem asserit."

had weakened his earlier phrasing of the argument and pressed home the point in all its strength. Here he uses a general negation, not a mere particular: "No affirmation can stand if part breaks down."[46] A proposition must stand as a whole in its subject and in its predicate. If Humbert sets up as his subject "the bread and wine of the altar," and as his predicate "are true Body and Blood of Christ," he cannot deny either term.[47] Berengar uses as an example the proposition, "Christus vincit." If the proposition is to stand as a whole, then "Christus" must stand and "vincit" must stand.[48]

Therefore, the formula as Humbert and Lanfranc understand it, ends in a contradiction in terms. If they hold that there is no bread on the altar after the Consecration, but only the Body of Christ, they are saying that that which no longer exists is something; they attempt to give some determination to nothingness, which is absurd. The rule of dialectics, closely related to Berengar's concept of being, is invincible:

> Whatever exists, is one thing in that it is, another in that it is something; and it cannot be anything if it does not exist.[49]

If the bread and wine of the altar are the true Body and Blood of Christ, the bread and wine remain. If you say Socrates is just, you say he is something; but he cannot be just if he does not exist.[50]

But Berengar does not entirely reject the proposition, "The bread and wine are the true Body and Blood of Christ." The proposition indeed is true, but not as Humbert and Lanfranc understand it. If a term is predicated of another term of which it is not predicable literally, the relation is therefore "tropical," or symbolical. In the Gospels, Christ is called lion, lamb, chief corner-stone, and the Apostle says that the

---

46 D.s.c., p. 211: "Omnis affirmatio non constabit parte subruta."

Cf. p. 234: "Omnis enuntiatio amissa parte altera utra, praedicatum dico atque subiectum, constare non poterit."

47 *Ibid.*, p. 107 f. Cf. pp. 30 f, 85.

48 *Ibid.*, p. 107: "Ita cum enuntiatio, quae dicit: Christus vincit, duas habeat partes, subiectum id, quod est Christus, praedicatum, quod est: vincit, quicumque mihi id totum dederit, quod est: Christus vincit, necessario ad eam partem, quae est Christus, et eam, quae est; vincit, dedisse convincitur."

49 *Ibid.*, p. 70: "verumque invincibiliter manet, omne, quod est, aliud est in eo, quod est, aliud in eo quod aliquid est, nec posse quippiam aliquid esse, cui contingat ipsum non esse."

50 *Ibid.*, "Ac per hoc cum dicitur, panis in altari consecratus . . . est Christi corpus, omni veritate panis superesse conceditur. Verbi gratia, si enuntias: Socrates iustus est, aliquid eum esse constitutisti, nec potest iustus esse, si contingat Socratem non esse."

rock was Christ; these predicates are all figures of speech.[51] Similarly, in the proposition, "The bread is the Body of Christ," there is a literal term and a figurative term, and the subject cannot be said to have passed out of existence.[52]

Some of the older Catholic writers, Mabillon, for example, have found in Berengar's readiness to accept the language of realism, indication that he accepted the doctrine of the real presence of Christ in the Eucharist, while he rejected substantial conversion. At the Synod of Tours, held in 1054 under the presidency of Hildebrand, he was permitted to swear to a realistic formula which contained no reference to the disappearance of the bread and wine. Berengar constantly affirmed that the bread and wine of the altar after Consecration are the Body and Blood of Christ.[53] He even spoke of a conversion as having taken place in the Eucharist. But he insists that there be careful understanding of what he means by conversion, since his interpretation is different from that of Lanfranc.[55] For Berengar, the conversion that takes place in the Eucharist is "through Consecration," and is closely connected with his theory of the sacrament.[56] The Eucharist through Consecration becomes the sanctifiying Body of Christ, but in no such way that the bread ceases to exist;[57] and after the Consecration, the

---

51 D.s.c., p. 83: "Constat enim apud eruditionem tuam, non minus tropica locutione dici: panis, qui ponitur in altari, post consecrationem est corpus Christi et vinum sanguis, quum dicitur: Christus est leo, Christus est agnus, Christus est summus angularis lapis, totique illi tropicae locutionis generi unum patere, non amplius, exitum."

Cf. pp. 84, 234, 279.

Cf. Ep. ad Adelm., Martène and Durand, *Thesaurus novus anecdotorum*, 4: 111B; 112A.

52 D.s.c., p. 70: "Utrumlibet horum concesseris, panem superesse post consecrationem in mensa dominica, omni procul dubio concessisti, multumque a seipso dissidet, qui dicit, panem in altari materialiter absumi."

53 *Ibid.*, p. 52: "Scripsi ergo ego ipse, quod iurarem: panis atque vinum altaris post consecrationem sunt corpus Christi et sanguis."

54 *Ibid.*, pp. 56-57: "Quod de conversione, . . . ego interim dico: panem et vinum per consecrationem converti in altari in verum Christi corpus et sanguinem."

55 *Ibid.*, p. 57: "Dum dicis, converti in veram Christi carnem et sanguinem, quam diceres conversionem, (est enim multiplex et vera conversio) minime assignasti."

56 *Ibid.*, p. 161: "Est ergo vero procul dubio panis et vini per consecrationem altaris conversio in corpus Christi et sanguinem, sed attendendum quod dicitur: per consecrationem, quia hic est huius conversionis modus."

57 *Ibid.*, p. 97: "Sed non ut ipse panis per corruptionem esse desinat panis, sed non ut corpus Chirsti nun incipiat per generationem sui, quia ante tot tempora beata constans immortalitate, non potest corpus illud etiam nunc incipere."

bread is called bread in a proper way of speaking, but the Body of Christ, "tropically," or figuratively.[58]

In spite of his protestations of belief in the presence of Christ in the Eucharist, it is clear therefore that he thought of the Eucharist as no more than a symbol of Christ's Body, which itself remains in heaven. Vernet suggests that in his earlier stage of development, Berengar held for a vague impanationism.[59] But this belief cannot be found in his developed thought. A presence of Christ's historical Body on the altar in some other way than through substantial change would be for him as contradictory as a presence through substantial change. The Body of Christ cannot possibly be in heaven and on earth at the same time. When we analyze Berengar's concept of the Eucharist as sacrament, we shall see more clearly the meaning of "conversion" in his understanding of the term; but it is sufficient to point out here that it involved no idea of Christ's real presence in the Eucharist beyond that of a symbol.

In the three arguments which have been analyzed consisted the substance of the Berengarian critique of the orthodox doctrine of substantial conversion. The latter two arguments are within the field of formal dialectics, the first in that border land where the pre-scholastic dialectics merged into immature metaphysical concepts. Berengar failed to achieve a true concept of the Holy Eucharist because his philosophy was unable to distinguish in a concrete object between its essential components and its non-essential qualities. This failure of his philosophy made the Eucharist an extremely difficult concept for him; but his rejection of the *magisterium* of the Church made him a heretic. It is true that during the pre-scholastic period the terms "materia" and "forma," "substantia" and "accidens," did not have the meaning which the Aristotelian metaphysics, as yet unknown, would give them. But the necessary distinctions were present in the traditional literature of the Eucharist, where a line had been drawn between the inner reality, which had been bread and wine, but which becomes the Body and Blood of Christ, and the accidental elements which remain.

But these distinctions were impossible in the philosophy of Berengar. In his identification of "accidens" with "forma," the accident is not a non-essential qualification of the subject, but enters into its essential

---

58 *Ibid.*, p. 87: ". . . ubi panem, qui proprie panis appelletur, corpus etiam Christi, sed tropica locutione, quantum ad eam propositionem, quae enuntiat: panis altaris post consecrationem est corpus Christi, nulla falsitate dissimulat appellari." Cf. p. 84.

59 "Bérenger de Tours," DTC 5: 727-728.

composition. Thus his philosophy is thoroughly sensist and empirical. Sensible experience is the only sure means of knowledge. Nothing exists except what can be seen and touched, and the senses perceive at once and directly not only the accidents, but the hidden reality in its entirely.[60]

Nearly all writers who have discussed the Berengarian controversy have pointed out the nominalist tendency in his philosophy—tendency, rather than actuality, since developed nominalism had not yet appeared. If the senses, which perceive only the particular, grasp nevertheless the total reality of being, then it would seem that for Berengar nothing is universal but all is individual. If the universal, then, has no reality, it becomes a mere concept, or perhaps a name. Doubtless Berengar did not advert to the general implications of his Eucharistic theory, and that is why some writers have spoken of a "special nominalism, limited to a single point."[61]

Some writers have seen in Berengar's sensism, combined with his thoroughgoing nationalism and rejection of traditional authority, a tendency towards skepticism, or the denial of mysterious elements in religion.[62] This does not seem entirely implausible.[63] If the real presence of Our Lord in the Eucharist is to be rejected because it is contrary to the evidence of the senses, then the doctrine of the hypostatic union might be rejected on similar grounds. If we are to trust Guitmund of Aversa, Berengar's insistence on the full corporality of the glorified

---

60 Clerval, *Les Écoles de Chartres*, pp. 119-120, notes that Berengar, in spite of his declarations upon the dignity of reason, is in reality as much opposed to reason as to authority: from intellectualism he passes to sensism.

Cf. Heitz, *Essai historique sur les rapports entre la philosophie et la foi, de Bérenger de Tours à S. Thomas d'Aquin*, p. 4; and Heurtevent, *op. cit.*, p. 42.

Cf. Guitmund, PL 149: 1485A: "Illi quippe judicium sensuum transcendere non valentes, tanquam ex infirmitate errasse videri possunt."

61 Vernet, DTC 5: 729, citing de Rémusat, *Abelard*, Paris, 1845, 1: 358: "un nominalisme spécial ou restraint à une seule question."

Harnack, *op. cit.*, p. 49, speaks of Berengar's nominalist tendency; admits the logical correctness of his position, but dismisses its metaphysical value with the comment, "Even Protestant historians will take no account of such reasons."

Geiselmann, *op. cit.*, p. 339, n. 1, speaks of Berengar's "covert nominalism."

Cf. Clerval, *op. cit.*, p. 120.

62 Faivre, E., *La question de l'autorité au moyen-age*, Paris, 1890, p. 37; Reuter, H., *Geschichte der religiösen Aufklärung in Mittelalter*, 2 vols., Berlin, 1875-1877, 1: 97.

63 Harnack, *op. cit.*, p. 46, and Macdonald, *op. cit.*, p. 303, n. 3, emphatically reject these suggestions of Faivre and Reuter. However, it is to the purpose of both Harnack and Macdonald to save Berengar's orthodoxy as a believer in revealed religion, while maintaining his separation from the Catholic Church.

Body of Christ led him to contradict the Gospel on at least one point:
that of the appearance of the Risen Lord to the Apostles *januis clausis*.[64]
Geiselmann says that Berengar rejected the doctrine of the preservation
of the integrity of Mary's body in the birth of Our Lord, in his conten-
tion that it would have been impossible for Christ to have been born
utero clauso.[65] But the attribution of further heresies to Berengar is
based at most on hints and rumors found in the writings of his contemporaries, and in certain obscure statements of his own. One can justi-
fiably speak only of a tendency towards skepticism, necessarily connected with his rationalism and his rejection of the authority of the
Church.

Berengar was of course wholly unjustified in his attribution to Paschasius and Lanfranc of the crudely materialistic theory of a real presence of portions of Christ's Body on the altar. Although Paschasius insisted on a physical presence, he was equally insistent on the spiritual
mode of that presence, and Lanfranc, Guitmund, and Alger, as we
shall see, were even more emphatic upon the integrity of Christ's Body
under the Eucharistic species. Berengar's misunderstanding is in large
part traceable to the language of the Humbertian formula of 1059:
". . . et sensualiter non solum sacramento, sed in veritate manibus sacerdotum tractari, frangi, et fidelium dentibus atteri." The language of
the formula was far from perfect: it provided ground for a capharnaitic misinterpretation of the traditional view, and it was entirely silent
upon the mode of the presence of Our Lord through a substantial conversion. But it was drawn up in such form precisely to prevent equivo-
cation by Berengar, who was always willing to swear to his belief that
the Body of Christ was really present, so long as this did not disturb the
continuance of the bread and wine.[66] The Anglican writer Darwell
Stone has pointed out that such realistic expressions as appear in the
formula of 1059 "were used by many as clumsy ways of expressing the

---

64 Guitmund, PL 149: 1480B: "Sed quid mirum, si Patrum historias Berengarius
et sui despiciunt qui Evangelio etiam contradicunt, dicentes nullatenus debere credi quod
ibi legitur intrasse ad discipulos Dominum Jesum *januis clausis* (Jn. 20: 19?")."

65 *Op. cit.*, p. 333. Cf. D.s.c., p. 290.
Macdonald, *op. cit.*, pp. 215-216, interprets Geiselmann as saying that Berengar
denied the virginal birth. Macdonald replies that Berengar had no intention to trifle
with this doctrine, but only to dismiss current errors which held Christ to have been
born as a developed man, in some miraculous way analogous to the formation of Eve
from Adam's side. But Geiselmann's point seems to deal with the virginal birth only in
the broad sense of the physical integrity of Mary not only *ante partum* but *in partum*.
Cf. Conc. Lateranense (649), DB 256.

66 See the luminous comment of St. Thomas on this formula in *Sum. Theol.*, 3,
q.77, a.7, ad 3.

conviction that the Sacrament which is so held and broken and crushed is the Body and Blood of Christ."[67]

2. *The Orthodox Rejoiner*

In this section, an effort will be made to develop the teaching of Lanfranc, Guitmund, and Alger concerning the doctrine of substantial conversion. The inquiry will be directed along three lines: first, the analysis of the conversion as it is found in these writers; second, their teaching concerning the condition of Christ's Body in the Eucharist; and third, their study of the Eucharistic accidents. In a certain sense, the three great anti-Berengarian writers may be handled collectively, since their teaching taken together represents the actual position of traditional theology at a critical moment of the history of dogma. But from another aspect, they must be studied individually, since at every point development may be seen among them: of Guitmund and Alger upon Lanfranc, and sometimes of Alger upon both of his predecessors. These points of development will be noted in the course of our study.

Further, the adversaries of Berengar will be studied here, not directly in the light of their patrology, which forms the greatest part of their work, but in that of dialectics; and our purpose will be to bring out the personal contribution which rational speculation enabled each of them to make to the deeper understanding of the traditional Eucharistic doctrine. This method of procedure is dictated by our general aim, which is to study the Berengarian controversy in the framework of pre-scholastic theology and the pre-scholastic method. But it is admittedly a partial study, and it has certain disadvantages.

In the first place, the Eucharistic theology of Berengar, as we have seen, is rooted in a philosophical error, his failure to see a real distinction between the corporeal substance and its accidents, and his consequent conviction that a separation of the two would be contradictory. But we will look in vain in Lanfranc, Guitmund, and Alger for a simply philosophical reply to this philosophical error. Their philosophy was not sufficiently advanced to set up such a thesis. For them the actual separation which takes place in the Eucharist is a fact contained

---

67 *A History of the Doctrine of the Holy Eucharist,* London, 1909, 2 vols., 1: 258.

Harnack, *op. cit.,* p. 47, n.2, is therefore unfair when he speaks of the proposition, "The Eucharist is the mystery (sacramentum) in which there is no mystery, but all takes place *vere et sensualiter,*" as representing "the fundamental thought of Berengar's opponents."

in Scripture and tradition, and taught by the Church. The philosophical truth that this actual separation, known by faith, was not contradictory to reason, was implicit in their teaching, and would not indeed become thoroughly explicit for a century or more after their time. It has been remarked already that it is thoroughly fair to Berengar to treat his Eucharistic theology exclusively from the viewpoint of dialectics. But this is not true of his adversaries. For them the argument from tradition is conclusive, and the chain of patristic evidence which they helped forge is even today of great value in showing the perennial constancy of the Catholic doctrines of the real presence and transubstantiation.

Moreover, it is somewhat unsatisfactory to handle the teaching of Lanfranc, Guitmund, and Alger as a collective response in controversy to the heresy of Berengar. Their writing lacks the direct point for point refutation that should be present in all controversial writing. Lanfranc alone attacks the heretic directly, citing him word for word. But his attack is directed against an earlier work, not the achieved doctrine of Berengar as we find it in the *De sacra coena*. And besides, his avowed reluctance to use dialectical arguments leads him to subside into silence before the actual end of inquiry has been reached. As for the successors of Lanfranc, although their treatises were written after the *De sacra coena* had appeared, yet they give no direct and undeniable evidence of having read it. The only citation of Berengar which appears in Alger of Liége is taken not from the *De sacra coena*, but from the earlier pamphlet, as Alger doubtless found it in Lanfranc's treatise.[68] And besides, both Guitmund and Alger wrote against a broader background, concerning themselves not merely with Berengar, but also with the "Berengariani," those mysterious disciples of Berengar who developed his teaching and refined it.[69]

There is, however, great value even in a partial study of these writers. In their Eucharistic doctrine, they carried the analysis of the doctrine of substantial conversion to a point appreciably in advance of the simpler formulas of the Fathers and of Paschasius Radbert; and through a more careful study of the mode of the real presence they effectually removed all carnal and capharnaitic elements from the realist doctrine as Berengar had misinterpreted it. In the broader framework of the history of theology, they stand at the gateway to developed scholasticism, and, in a context of the greatest theological importance, they provide a passage

---

68 Alg., PL 180: 791 CD-Lanf., PL 150: 436A.
69 See, for example, Guit., PL 149: 1430 CD; Alg., PL 180: 739 D-740 B.

between the conservative tradition which preceded them, and the great progress which was to follow.

With the range of inquiry thus marked out, it is to the purpose now to study our authors' analysis of the Catholic doctrine of substantial conversion. The term "substantial conversion" is used throughout, because of course "transubstantiation" does not yet exist in the language of Eucharistic theology. However, if the term itself is lacking, the concept of transubstantiation is clearly contained in the writings of Lanfranc, Guitmund, and Alger. They hold it to be the faith of the Church throughout the world that bread and wine are placed on the altar to be consecrated; but in the course of the consecration these elements are incomprehensibly and ineffably changed into the substance of the Body and Blood of Christ,[70] the same Body which was born of the Virgin,[71] and which hung upon the Cross.[72] In their abundant formulations of the doctrine of substantial conversion, various terms are used to designate the change. The bread and wine are "transferred" into Christ; they are "transformed," "converted," "substantially changed" into the Flesh and Blood of Christ.[73] The change operates so that after it takes place the elements cease to be what they were;[74] and the change is effected in the consecration, through the priestly benediction.[75]

But the substantial conversion which takes place in the Eucharist affects only the inner reality of the sacramental elements; the external species, or appearances, remain unchanged. In distinguishing the sacramental reality from the species, our authors make use of a text, which had also been used by Berengar, from the Ambrosian *De sacramentis:* "ut sint quae erant, et in aliud commutentur."[76] Berengar had taken this to mean that the bread and wine remain what they were essentially,

---

70 Lanf., 419 A: "Confitetur enim Ecclesia, toto terrarum orbe diffusa, panem et vinum ad sacrandum, incomprehensibiliter et ineffabiliter *in substantiam* carnis et sanguinis commutari."

71 *Ibid.,* 415 A.

72 *Ibid.,* 428 B.

73 Guit., PL 149: 1436 B: "Christus panem et vinum . . . transferre in corpus et sanguinem suum." Cf. 1431 C.

Ibid., 1431 D: "ut videlicet in carnem et sanguinem suum panem vinumque transformet."

Guit., PL 149: 1488 B: "Sed panem et vinum altaris Domini in corpus et sanguinem Christi substantialiter commutari."

Alg., PL 180: 741 B: "qui elementa bruta panis et vini in suam convertit substantiam."

74 Alg., 808 C: "Panis enim et vini substantia in corpus et sanguinem Christi conversa, dum facta est quod non erat, desistit esse quod fuerat."

75 Lanf., 423 C: "Inter sacrandum vero converti in Christi carnem et sanguinem, quas utrasque res benedictio consecravit."

but acquire new value by becoming a sacrament, a symbol of Christ's Body. Against this new interpretation, Lanfranc argues that no one in his right mind could believe that a thing could be changed into something else without ceasing to be what it was.[77] Then he sets down the traditional interpretation:

> [Ambrose] testifies that they remain what they were in their visible appearance, but that they are changed in their inner essence into the nature of those things which they had not been before.[78]

Alger of Liége is subtler than Lanfranc in discussing the same text. Lanfranc had simply asked how a thing could change and remain the same. But Alter distinguishes a substantial change from an accidental change.[79] And since in the Eucharist the accidents do not change, but remain the same, therefore it is the substance of bread which ceases to be.[80] His explanation of the passage is then the same as that of Lanfranc, with some variation of terminology.[81]

The most complete statement of the orthodox doctrine of substantial conversion is contained in the long profession of faith of Lanfranc:

> We believe, therefore, that the earthly substances upon the table of the Lord are divinely sanctified through the priestly mystery and the divine power, and are ineffably, incomprehensibly, and marvellously changed into the essence of the Body of the Lord. The former appearances and certain other qualities remain, that recipients may not refrain from receiving through horror and disgust, and that believers may attain to the ampler rewards of faith. Meanwhile the Body of the Lord remains in heaven at the right hand of the Father, immortal, inviolate, entire, untouched, and unhurt. And so, the Body of Christ on the altar may be called the same Body which was born of the Virgin, and not the same. It is the same in essence, and in the propriety and power of its true nature; it is not the same if considered in its appearances of bread

---

76 *Supra*, p. 46.

77 Lanf., 419 D: "Quis enim compos sui credit rem aliquam converti in aliam, nec tamen in ea parte desinere esse quod erat?"

78 *Ibid.*, 420 D: "Esse quidem secundum visibilem speciem testatur quae erant, commutari vero secundum interiorem *essentiam* in naturam illarum rerum quae antea non erant."

79 PL 180: 756 D: "Quidquid enim mutatur in aliud, in aliquo desinit esse quod fuerat sive substantialiter, sive accidentaliter."

80 *Ibid.*, 757 A: "Sed in pane et vino cum in corpus Christi mutantur, accidentia esse non desinunt, sed omnia remanent: ergo panis et vini substantia esse desinit."

81 *Ibid.*, 756 D: "secundum formam et caeteras suas qualitates ibidem remanentes, et secundum substantiam in aliud mutentur."

Note that Alger, like Berengar, uses "forma" as synonymous with "accidens," but of course without holding it to be inseparable from substance.

and wine, and the other qualities mentioned above. This faith the Catholic and universal Church has held from the earliest times, and holds now.[82]

In this excellent formula is seen the chief contribution of Lanfranc to the literature of the controversy. It contains in summary fashion the doctrine of substantial conversion and the permanence of the accidents; it effectively repudiates any capharnaitic interpretation by distinguishing two modes of being of the Body of Christ, the natural and the sacramental. And finally, it is set forth not as an opinion, but as a dogma of the Catholic Church. Thus, Lanfranc charts the course, lays out the field of inquiry; and every point of development in Guitmund and Alger will be within the area marked out in Lanfranc's profession of faith. But the mere statement of his faith marks the end of inquiry for Lanfranc. He will not push his investigations any further. How bread and wine can be changed into Flesh and Blood; how the nature of the two elements can be essentially changed, are mysteries of faith: the just man does not seek to inquire into them.[83] It is enough for Lanfranc to say that the divine omnipotence, operating miraculously, can effect such a marvellous change.[84]

Both Guitmund and Alger attempt to analyze the change, however. Guitmund's procedure is first to refute the theory of impanationism, which would hold that both the substance of bread and the substance of Christ's Body are present in the consecrated Host. Such a theory is contrary to reason, to the institution of Christ, to the apostolic preaching, and to the universal consent of the faithful.[85] It is revealed, not

---

82 Lanf., 430 C: "Credimus igitur terrenas substantias, quae in mensa Dominica, per sacerdotale mysterium, divinitus sanctificantur, ineffabiliter, incomprehensibiliter, mirabiliter, operante superna potentia, converti in essentiam Dominici corporis, reservatis ipsarum rerum speciebus, et quibusdam aliis qualitatibus, ne percipientes cruda et cruenta, horrerent, et ut credentes fidei praemia ampliora perciperent, ipso tamen Dominico corpore existente in coelestibus ad dextream Patris, immortali, inviolato, integro incontaminato, illaeso; ut vere dici possit, et ipsum corpus quod de virgine sumptum sumere, et tamen non ipsum. Ipsum quidem, quantum ad essentiam veraeque naturae proprietatem atque virtutem; non ipsum autem, si species panis vinique speciem, caeteraque superius comprehense; hanc fidem tenuit a priscis temporibus, et nunc tenet Ecclesia, quae per totum diffusa orbem catholica nominatur."

83 Lanf., 427 A: "Quonamodo panis efficiatur caro vinumque convertatur in sanguinem, utriusque essentialiter mutata natura, justus, qui ex fide vivit, scrutari argumentis et concipere ratione non quaerit."

84 *Ibid.*, "Divina tamen potentia mirabiliter operante fieri posse concedit."

85 Guit., PL 149: 142 B: "At impanari vel invinari Christum nulla . . . expetit ratio, nec prophetae praedixerunt, nec Christus ostendit, nec apostoli praedicaverunt, nec mundus, exceptis his paucissimus haereticis, credidit."

that the Body and Blood of the Lord lie hidden in the bread and wine, but that the bread and wine are changed into the Body and Blood.[86]

Besides rejecting impanationism as an explanation of the real presence, Guitmund enters upon a deeper penetration through an analysis of the concept of change. Berenger also had done this; but it is significant that whereas Berengar's analysis was based on the distinctions found in the dialectical tradition, Guitmund's is founded on Scripture.[87] The first three kinds of change noted by Guitmund correspond to the "generatio subiecti," "corruptio subiecti," and subiectum in subiectum" of Berengar.[88] But there is a fourth type of conversion, altogether unique and known by faith, in which that which exists is changed into something which is already in existence—the process in which bread and wine are changed into the Body and Blood of Christ.[89]

Guitmund then sets up a claim that the Eucharistic conversion, though mysterious, is easier for us to believe than either creation or annihilation, since it involves two terms instead of only one.[90] Thus the Eucharist is more closely akin to the third type of change, the "subjectum in subjectum," which is most familiar to us. And he concludes that if God can create, if He can annihilate—acts extremely difficult for us to understand; then we ought also to believe Him able, if He wills, to effect a change which seems easier for us to understand.[91]

---

86 *Ibid.*, 1482: ". . . non in pane et vino corpus et sanguinem Domini latere, sed panem et vinum in corpus et sanguinem Domini commutari docuit."

87 *Ibid.*, 1443 C: "Quattuor enim . . . rerum mutationes substantivas sive efficientias nobis Scriptura divina commendat."

88 *Ibid.*, 1443 C: "omnino nihil in id quod sunt;" "de eo quod sunt . . . redire in nihilum possunt;" 1444 B: "substantiae in eas quae non erant substantias . . . transeunt."

89 *Ibid.*, 1444 B: "Quarta vero mutatio est, quia id quod est transit in id quod nihilominus est, sicut panem et vinum virtute divina in corpus Christi proprium singulari potentia credimus commutari."

90 *Ibid.*, 1444 C: "Illae enim duo aliqua habet; istae unum tantum."

91 Guit., 1444 C: "illi quae usitatissima est, multo vicinior atque similior."

Ibid., 1445 A: "facilius et intelligibilius si voluit, fecit."

Billot, *De Ecclesiae Sacramentis*, 1, ed. 6, Rome, 1924, p. 368, says transubstantiation is a more difficult truth than creation: in the latter, no positive contrary consideration enters in to hinder assent, but there is lacking only a similar example; in the former, however, there is a positive consideration contrary to our experience: that one subject changes into another without any essential principle remaining common to both subjects.

Alger of Liége also carries the analysis of the substantial change considerably farther than Lanfranc. First he distinguishes the Eucharist from Baptism and Confirmation. These two sacraments do not possess Christ substantially, but only in His power. Only the sacrament of the bread and wine is so changed as substantially to cease to be what it was; its substance becomes the Body of Christ, while its form remains, and signifies the Body of Christ and contains it.[92]

Alger then rejects the theory of those who hold that Christ assumes the appearance or form of bread on the altar, as the divine Word assumed the appearance or form of flesh in the virginal womb: as the Word was made Flesh, so is bread made the same Flesh. Alger, too, holds that the Word was made Flesh, and the bread becomes the same Flesh, but in a vastly different way:

> The Word was made Flesh, and was born, flesh from flesh; the Word assumed flesh, it was not changed into flesh. It became what it had not been before, without ceasing to be what it was. But bread becomes the same Flesh: it is not born as flesh, nor does it assume flesh, but is changed into flesh. It becomes what it had not been before, in such a way as to cease to be what it was.[93]

Moreover, in the virginal womb, the divine Word assumed the appearance or form of flesh along with the substance, while on the altar, the substance alone of the bread is changed, while its appearance or form remains.[94]

Further, Alger distinguishes the Eucharistic change from the natural change which takes place when food is brought into the body. In this he is opposing the singular conception of those who held that the eucharistic bread is changed into "new flesh" of Christ, as ordinary food is changed into bodily tissue. But the change which takes place in the Eucharist *per gratiam* is far different from that which takes place

---

92 Alg., PL 180: 761 A: "ita mutatur, ut substantialiter sit quod ante fuerat; sed substantia eius corpus Christi fiat, forma vero remanens ipsum significet et contineat."

93 *Ibid.*, 755 AB: "Revera enim Verbum fit caro, et panis fit eadem caro; sed longe diverso modo. Verbum fit caro, et nascitur caro de carne, assumendo carnem, non mutatum in carnem: sic factum quod non fuerat, ut non desisteret esse quod erat. Panis autem fit eadem caro, non nascitur caro, nec assumit carnem, sed mutatur in carnem; sic factus quod non erat, ut desistat esse quod fuerit."

94 *Ibid.*, 755 CD: "cum in utero sumpserit speciem vel formam cum substantia, in altari vero speciem vel formam panis mutata et non permanente substantia."

per naturam. For in the digestive process, says Alger, even as it concerned the natural Body of Christ on earth, food is changed into new
flesh, not through a change of substance but of form, and the flesh
which results is natural flesh, subject to corruption.[95] And he continues,

> But in the sacrament of the altar, the substance is changed and not
> the form, the bread and wine do not become new flesh; but the existing
> substance of bread and wine is changed into the pre-existing substance
> of the Body of Christ.[96]

And Alger adds the important note that the "novelty" which befalls the
bread in no way entails newness of existence on the part of Christ, and
the change in the bread causes no change in Christ.[97]

Thus, there is involved in this rejection of a ridiculous error an important clarification of the doctrine of transubstantiation—namely that
in the eucharistic conversion the entire action is exercised on the bread;
no action is exercised on Christ's Body: no "bringing" of Christ to the
altar, no "production" or "reproduction" of Christ's Body on the
altar.[98]

Alger's positive analysis of the substantial conversion is based on
the *De mysteriis* of St. Ambrose.[99]   In Chapter 9, Ambrose, wishing to
illustrate the eucharistic change, had made use of Old Testament analogies.   Moses had held a rod and it became a serpent; he touched a
rock and water gushed forth.   St. Ambrose argues that if the human
benediction of Moses was so powerful as to change the nature of things,
how much more powerful must be the divine consecration effected
through the words of Christ.   Further, the *sermo Christi* was able to

---

95 *Ibid.*, 766 C: "In stomacho enim Christi panis et vinum, non mutata vel defici-
ente substantia, sed forma, novam carnem et novum sanguinem, corruptioni aliquatenus
obnoxium, sicut in caeteris hominibus generavit."

Here it should be noted that Alger does not mean to deny that in a natural transformation the form alone, i.e. the accidents, are changed. He only means to point out
that in every natural transformation something of the transformed element subsists, the
terminus a quo never disappears completely. While in the Eucharist, on the contrary,
only the appearances of bread and wine remain. Cf. Brigué, *Alger de Liége*, p. 81.

96 *Ibid.*, "in sacramento autem, mutata substantia non forma, panis et vinum non fit
nova caro et novus sanguis, sed existens substantia panis et vini mutatur in coexistentem
substantiam corporis Christi."

97 Alg., 766 C: "ita ut novitate sua nihil in ipso innovat, mutatione sua nihil
immutet."

98 Cf. de la Taille, *op. cit.*, p. 637, Billot, *op. cit.*, pp. 346-349. Alger's teaching
here contains that "purity" of concept of transubstantiation, which was current among
the "veteres scholastici," and which Billott and de la Taille have emphasized, as opposed
to the complicated processes of certain "recentiores."

create all things from nothing; it should also be able to perform the lesser marvel of changing the natures of things which exist already. And Ambrose concludes, with regard to the Eucharist: "Et hoc quod conficimus ex virgine est."

Alger says that Ambrose has distinguished three types of divine activity: creation, mutation, and the eucharistic conversion. God has ceased creating;[100] He has communicated to creatures as secondary causes the power to effect substantial changes through a change of form (mutation);[101] the third change, entirely unique, is exclusively the prerogative of the divine word spoken in consecration:[102]

> The Body of Christ in the sacrament is not believed to be created, as in the primary origin of nature; nor is the bread changed in form, as in the usual process which God has communicated to nature; but in an entirely new and unheard of way the substance of bread is so changed into the substance of the Body of Christ as to cease to be bread, except in appearance, while the Body of Christ remains entirely unchanged.[103]

Thus it is clear that Alger of Liége has carried the analysis of the substantial conversion to a point of development considerably in advance of Lanfranc and even of Guitmund. He has refuted impanationism, has distinguished the eucharistic conversion from creation and from natural processes of change which are effected through a change of form, and has emphasized the fact that the change affects the bread only and not at all the Body of Christ. It is only then that Alger, as Lanfranc had done at a much earlier stage in the inquiry, sets a limit to rational investigation. If one seeks to know how a corruptible thing can be changed into an incorruptible thing; an existing thing into a preexisting Body;[104] how the new can be changed into the old without

---

99 J. Quasten, ed., *Monumenta eucharistica et liturgica vetustissima,* Pars III. (Florilegium Patristicum, Fasc. 7), Bonn, 1936, pp. 133-135.

100 Alg. PL 180; 768 A: "quorum quia ab altero quievit."

101 *Ibid.,* "alterum naturae communicavit."

102 *Ibid.,* "Tertium privilegium divini sermonis adscribens subiecit."

103 *Ibid.,* 786 AB: "Nec de nihilo credatur corpus Christi creari in sacramento, secundum primariae naturae originem, nec panis formam mutari secundum naturae communictam consuetudinem; sed novo et inaudito modo ita mutari substantiam panis in substantiam corporis Christi, ut panis non sit, sed appareat esse quod fuerat, et corpus Christi non desistat esse quod erat."

For an analysis of Berengar's explanation of the same Ambrosian passage, see Schnitzer, *Berengar von Tours,* p. 291. Berengar twisted the clear meaning of Ambrose beyond all recognition.

104 *Ibid.,* 766 D: "Existens in coexistentem."

change or innovation of the latter;[105] the answer must be that these things are part of the mystery of faith. And Alger cites Lanfranc's words, which he attributes, however, to Augustine, "in libro Sententiarum Prosperi." [106]

In answer to the crudity of Berengar's conception of the realist doctrine of the real presence, Lanfranc, Guitmund, and Alger made important contributions to the better understanding of the actual condition of Christ's Body in the Eucharist. Berengar had held that the idea of a physical presence of Christ upon the altar necessarily involved an absurd multi-locality of Christ's Body and the denial of His continued presence in heaven in glory until the end of time. Moreover, the opinion which Berengar attributed to his opponents of a presence of little portions of the Body would destroy the impassibility of Christ's glorified Body.

In opposition to these views, it was the work of Lanfranc, as usual, to lay the groundwork for development by pointing out that the presence, though real and substantial, is entirely invisible and spiritual; and that Christ's presence on earth does not at all conflict with His incorruptible life in heaven. Lanfranc places the fundamental distinction between the visible thing which is seen, the species of bread and wine, and the invisible reality which is adored, the Flesh and Blood of Christ.[107] The error of the people of Capharnaum, says Lanfranc, lay in the fact that they failed to make this distinction. They thought that the Lord commanded them to eat, in the ordinary way, the Flesh which they saw, and to drink the Blood which His persecutors were to shed.[108] This misapprehension the Lord reproved when He told them that the spirit gives life while the flesh profits nothing. The Body of Christ in the Eucharist is not the object of sense perception. What is seen is the corporeal species, but what is adored is Christ.

And because the eucharistic presence is spiritual and invisible, it is entirely compatible with Christ's remaining in the glory of heaven

---

105 *Ibid.*, "nova in antiquam sine illius innovatione vel mutatione."

106 *Ibid.*: "respondet tibi Augustinus in libro sententiarum Prosperi: 'si quaeris modum quo id possit fieri, breviter ad praesens respondeo: mysterium fidei est, credi salubriter potest, investigari utiliter non potest.'"

107 Lanf., PL 150: 423 C: "Nos etenim in specie panis et vini quam videmus, res invisibiles, id est Christi carnem et sanguinem, honoramus."

Cf. 421 B, and Alg., PL 180: 772 A, C; 820 D.

108 Lanf., PL 150: 434 B: "aut bestiali more, aut humano, corpus comedere quod videbant, aut bibere sanguinem quem persequentes fusuri erant."

until the end of time.[109]   In the earlier treatise, Berengar had objected that if the bread is changed into Christ's Body, then either the bread must be raised up to heaven or the Body must come down to earth. Lanfranc refuses to accept the dilemma, but characteristically makes no attempt to penetrate into the question raised.   How it is possible that Christ can be in heaven and on earth at the same time is an impenetrable mystery; Berengar's objection is based on human wisdom, not divine.[110]

But Alger of Liége makes some attempt to solve the problem of the twofold presence.   In the first place, he recognizes the existence of the problem when he says that every corporeal object must be related to a place.   But he rejects the Berengarian view that the Body of Christ in its present state is fully corporeal and in every way subject to the laws of space.   Even our own bodies after the resurrection will be endowed with remarkable spirituality and agility, free from the sluggishness of movement which afflicts us now.[112]   If this will be true of ourselves, it is even now much more true of the glorified Body of the omnipotent Christ, our Head.

But if from the argument so far one might conclude that Alger held for a presence by local motion, he quickly repudiates the idea.   No glorified body—not even the Body of Christ in its natural state—can pass from one place to another without leaving the place where it was.[113]   Christ is present in the Eucharist, not by passing from place to place, but remaining where He was, He wills to be on earth also in the sacrament.   He is present, wholly, entirely, and substantially, in heaven and on earth.[114]

The simultaneous presence of a body in many places would be contradictory if all the presences were held to be formally identical.   Alger escapes the contradiction by distinguishing two different modes of being of the Body of Christ; the human form and the sacramental form.   This

---

109 *Ibid.*, 422 B: "Procul avertat Deus ab Ecclesia sua talem sententiam [Capharnaiticam] : Sic nempe in terris immolatum Christum manducamus et bibimus, ut in coelestibus ad dexteram Patris integer semper existat et vivus."

Cf. 421 D, 427 C, 430 C; Alg., 780 C, D.

110 *Ibid.*, 439 C: "secundum humanam sapientiam, non secundum divinam."

111 Alg., PL 180: 780 C: "Quamvis enim omne corpus, omnisque creatura localis sit."

781 A: "ipsamque carnem, cum sit localis."

112 *Ibid.*, 782 B: "nulla sua tarditate impediantur."

113 *Ibid.*, 782 C: "ut inde recedit unde remaneat."

114 *Ibid.*, "Non de loco ad locum transeundo sed ibi, ubi est remanendo, et alibi . . . existendo, tota et integra, et substantialiter sit et in coelo et in terra."

distinction had been made without particular stress by Lanfranc in his long profession of faith, but Alger emphasizes it and illustrates it. At the Last Supper, Christ, in human form, gave His Body to the disciples in sacramental form.[115]   Thus the Body which they received from His hands was identical with the Body of Christ which stood before them, and at the same time it was different.[116]   Today He is in heaven in that human form in which He appeared before the disciples, but whether in the human form or in the sacramental form, it is the same Christ in both places, in heaven and on earth.[117]

Guitmund of Aversa contributed to the study of the character of the eucharistic presence explicit statements of the integrity of Christ's Body in the Host. Contrary to the opinion of Berengar, the realists did not hold for a presence of portions of Christ's Body, but a presence whole and entire:

> The whole Host is the Body of Christ, in such a way, however, that each separate particle is the whole Body of Christ. And three separated particles are not three Bodies, but one Body.[118]

Guitmund uses Berengar's word "portiuncula," but in such a way as to preclude any capharnaitic interpretation.[119]   If one communicant receives Holy Communion, he receives the entire Body of Christ; if two receive, or if many receive, all receive the same Body without distinction.[120]   And Guitmund adds that this is true even though a thousand Masses be celebrated at the same time,[121] in answer, perhaps, to the attempted *reductio in absurdum* placed by Berengar in the *De sacra coena*. Guitmund uses an analogy drawn from human speech to illustrate the

---

115 *Ibid.*, 781 B: "forma illa humana, in qua Christus, coenans cum discipulis, tradidit illis seipsum in sacramento."

116 *Ibid.*, "quasi alium et tamen eundem."

117 *Ibid.*, "uno loco est in coelis ad dexteram Patris integra, sicut integra fuit in coena, quando in sacramento comedebatur a discipulis; et tamen et in humana, et in sacramentali forma, idem verus utrobique Christus, et in coelo et in terris."

Cf. Conc. trid., Sess. XIII, Cap. I, DB 874: "Ad dextram Patris in coelis assideat iuxta modum existendi naturalem, et ut multis nihilominus aliis in locis sacramentaliter praesens."

118 Guit., PL 149: 1434 A: "Ita ergo tota hostia est corpus Christi, ut nihilominus unaquaeque particula separata sit totum corpus Christi. Nec tamen tres particulae separatae sunt tria corpora, sed unum corpus."

Cf. Alg., PL 180: 783 AB.

119 *Ibid.*, "Possumus quoque dicere tantumdem esse in una quasi portiuncula quantum erat in hostia tota."

120 Guit., PL 149, 1434 D: "Totum unus, totum duo, totum plures, sine diminutione percipiunt."

121 *Ibid.*, "Idem quoque dicimus, etsi mille missae eodem tempore celebrentur."

In this comment is found one of a few scattered hints that Guitmund might have read the *De sacra coena*.

totality of Christ's presence in heaven and in the consecrated Host. We know by daily experience that it is possible for us to express a thought to many at the same time and yet retain it whole and entire within our own mind. And even though we have many hearers, all receive the same word.[122] If this is so of the frail and transitory word of man, it is much more so of the unique and coeternal Word of the omnipotent God, that He can share Himself with many, and yet remain whole and entire and unchanged, in heaven. Guitmund does not claim that his argument explains the mystery, but asserts only that it serves to make the mystery credible, or not incredible.[123]

The important question of concomitance is raised by the twofold consecration of the Eucharistic species, the bread into the Body and the wine into the Blood. Does this mean that Christ is only partially present under each species? Lanfranc speaks of the condition of Christ's Body in the Eucharist as if he thought that under the species of bread only the Body is found, and under the species of wine only the Blood.[124] Guitmund surely understood the doctrine correctly, but his references are only to the totality of Christ's presence under the consecrated Host.[125] But Alger is the first to affirm explicitly the doctrine of concomitance, by placing a distinction which would enter into the official teaching of *magisterium* at the Council of Trent.[126] Alger introduces the problem in the form of a question:

> The question is raised why the bread is consecrated into Flesh and the wine into Blood, in such a way that the former is called Flesh *per se*, and the latter Blood *per se*, when the whole Christ is received in the Flesh and the whole Christ in the Blood, and there are not two Christs divided, but one sole Christ under each species.[127]

In this passage it is clear that Alger's distinction is precisely the same

---

122 Guit., 1435 B: "ut qui in corde nostro latens nobis solus cognitus erat, per vocem aliis etiam manifestari possit eodem tempore et totus in corde nostro remanet, et totus aeque mille hominibus cum assumpta voce sua quantum in se est, ita apparere potest."

Cf. Alg., 784 C:

123 *Ibid.*, 1435 C: "et si capere non posset, habere incredibile [nemo] debet."

124 PL 150: 428 B, 414 B.

Cf. Amann and Gaudel, "Lanfranc," DTC 8: 2659.

125 Guit., 1433 C, D.

126 Conc. trid., Sess. XIII, Cap. 3, DB 876, and cn. 3, DB 885.

127 Alg., PL 180: 825 D—826 A: "Quaeritur quoque quare panis in carnem, vinum in sanguinem per se consecrentur, ut illud per se caro, et illud per se sanguis dicatur, cum in carne totus Christus, et in sanguine totus Christus sumi credatur, nec tamen divisim duo Christi, sed in utroque unus solus Christus?"

as that which the Council of Trent will place, with the substitution of the term, "vi verborum," for Alger's "caro et sanguis per se." And Alger answers his question by saying that the double consecration is performed in this way for two reasons: in imitation of the practice of Christ Himself at the Last Supper,[128] and in connection with the Catholic doctrine of the Eucharist as sacrament and sacrifice.[129] When the species of bread is torn with the teeth, the Body of Christ broken in the Passion is signified; and when the species of wine is received into the mouths of the faithful, it is a figure of the Blood flowing from Christ's side.[130] Thus Alger properly relates the duality of the Eucharistic species to the Passion of Christ as a sign; yet it must be noted that he considers this significance not with reference to the consecration itself, but to the communion of priest and people.

In summary, there is a notable development among the anti-Berengarian writers in the delineation of the character of the real presence. Lanfranc denied any conflict between the simultaneous presence of Christ in heaven and in the Eucharist, but regarded it as an impenetrable mystery; while Alger makes a real contribution in the distinction between the two modes, or forms, of being, the "forma humana" and the "forma sacramentalis." Guitmund shows that the gross misunderstanding of Berengar—the "portiuncula carnis"—is entirely out of accord with the traditional doctrine, by insisting that Christ is present whole and entire even under the divided species; and Alger in turn follows with an explicit statement of the important doctrine of concomitance.

The mystery remains,[131] but real progress has been made. The ultimate explanation can only be found in the omnipotent divine will. In this connection, finally, Alger more than once distinguishes a twofold omnipotence in Christ, one by reason of His Divinity, the divine power of the Incarnate Word, and the other even in His Humanity: for to Him all power has been given in heaven and on earth.[132]

---

128 *Ibid.*, 826 A: "quia iste mos inolevit in Ecclesia ab ipso Christo, qui corpus sum et sanguinem divisim consecravit et dedit."

129 *Ibid.*, "ad discretionem figurae."

130 *Ibid.*, "ut panis dum dentibus teritur, carnem Christi in passione attritam, et dum vinum in ore fidelium funditur, sanguinem de latere Christi fusum signaret." Cf. 826 B, C, 785 C.

131 *Ibid.*, 783 B: "Quomodo tamen corpus Christi et coelo et mundo praesens, et dividatur indivisum et sumatur inconsumptum ratio stupet, fides ipsa miratur."

132 Alg., PL 180: 783 B: "Sed ex adjunctae divinitatis potentia quae ubique tota-praesens est in corpore suo spirituali, imo per omnipotentiam sibi collatam; divino iam facto id fieri posse, non diffidens veneratur." Cf. 785 B: "omnipotentiae, quae Christo etiam pro carnis parte collata est." 782 BC, 783 B.

The objective reality of the accidents of bread and wine is an essential element in the Catholic doctrine of the Real Presence. Previous to the eleventh century little study had been made of the Eucharistic species as such: pre-scholastic writers were content to say that one must not judge of the reality from what appears to the senses. In the Eucharist, one thing is seen, another is believed. But Lanfranc, Guitmund, and Alger, induced perhaps by Berengar's identification of the sensible phenomena with the total reality, treat specially of the eucharistic accidents. Beyond the simple question of the fact of the permanence of the accidents, two other questions are principally involved. The first concerns the real existence of the accidents after consecration, and the second concerns the corruption of the accidents, either through digestion, profanation, or similar process. Alger of Liége discusses the first of these two questions in language which later scholasticism will hardly improve; but in reply to the second question both Guitmund and Alger fall into a curious error which subsequent writers will correct.

It is settled that the opponents of Berengar held that the total reality of the bread and wine is changed into the total reality of the Body and Blood. After the consecration, there is no bread on the Altar, but only the Body of Christ.[133] Yet something remains of the bread, not its substance, its reality, but certain non-essential properties distinct from the reality and actually separated from it. These residual elements of the bread and wine are given a variety of designations. Lanfranc refers to the "species" of bread and wine, and certain other "qualities." The terminology of Alger in this matter is strongly influenced by that of Lanfranc. He also speaks of the "species" of bread and wine, the "qualities," and he describes the qualities as "accidental." Alger, like Berengar, uses the term "forma" to characterize the eucharistic accidents, without however identifying "forma" so understood with the essential constituents of the subject. Guitmund's terminology is more advanced than that of Lanfranc and Alger. Besides using their terms, he adopts the language which will become fixed in scholastic terminology: the accidents of bread and wine remain.[134]

---

133 *Ibid.*, 755 D: "Panis enim et vinum in sacramento jam non sunt, sed ante fuerunt."

134 Lanf., PL 150: 430 C: "reservatis ipsarum rerum speciebus, et quibusdam aliis qualitatibus."

Cf. 424 B, 416 C; Alg., PL 180: 755 D, 760 B, 809 B; Guit., PL 149: 1450 A. Alg., 809 D: "accidentales qualitates;" 755 D: "species vel forma panis et vini;" 759 C: "forma panis."

Guit., 1481 B: "caetera quaedam accidentia;" 1450 B: "ipsa accidentia."

Notwithstanding differences of terminology, all three agree in their teaching. "Species," "forma," "qualities," "accidents," all mean the same thing: the appearances which remain on the altar after the substantial conversion has taken place. If the sacred writings sometimes refer to the Eucharist as "bread" even after the consecration, this is not a substantial but a figurative predication. The sacrament is "confected" from bread and retains some of its qualities;[135] moreover it is the bread of eternal life and the bread of angels.[136]

Lanfranc and Guitmund did not discuss the reality of the eucharistic accidents beyond stating the mere fact of their permanence. Alger, on the other hand, contributes the valuable teaching that the accidents remain as accidents *per se* without a subject. The senses are not deceived in the Eucharist:

> The sacrifice of the Church . . . contains truly and naturally the Body and Blood of Christ, but also truly and naturally the appearance of the elements which were before.[137]

Alger entirely rejects the idea of a phantasmal presence of the accidents.[138] That which is present upon the altar is real; any other conclusion would be contrary to reason. We must hold for the reality of the sacramental appearances, for the merit of faith would be lessened if the bread wholly vanished from the altar; and something visible and real is necessary for the eucharistic sacrifice and for Holy Communion.[139]

But if the appearance of bread and wine are real, and if they are accidents, then in what subject do they exist? This is a question which "dialecticians" would raise, and Alger introduces his solution by a reference to the dialecticians of his day:

> But the dialecticians ask, if the substance of bread is changed into the Body of Christ, so that there is no longer any bread, in what subject then do these qualities remain that they should retain the color and

---

135 Alg., 755 D: "ex eo conficitur, ejusque nonnullas retinet qualitates." The term "conficitur" is easily understood, but cannot well be translated into English.

136 *Ibid.*

137 *Ibid.*, 760 B: "Sacrificium enim Ecclesiae . . . vere et naturaliter continet corpus Christi et sanguinem, et nihilominus vere et naturaliter elementorum eamdem fuerat speciem."

138 *Ibid.*, 759 D: "Phantastica enim illusio magicis congruit et diabolicis fraudibus." Cf. 758 D.

139 *Ibid.*, 758 D: "Non enim superesset aliquid visibile, circa quod mystica passionis signa . . . compleri, vel infirmis viaticum dari; nec caetera quae visibiliter et salubriter . . . valerent administrari."
Cf. 759 BC.

taste of bread, since the substance of the sacrament itself, that is, the Body of Christ, neither looks like bread nor tastes like bread? The answer to this question is that as God is marvellous in all things, so is He in this. He causes the accidental qualities in His sacrament to exist of themselves, which in other things is impossible.[140]

In no other matter, perhaps, does Alger show himself so far in advance of earlier writers. They had discussed the permanence of the species only in general terms, without analysis, often in such a way as to give the impression that the senses are somehow deceived in the Eucharist. But Alger sets out the problem in philosophical language ("in quo fundamento remanent qualitates?") and solves it in the same terms that will prevail in the schools.[141]

Although Guitmund and Alger were always careful to avoid confusion between the invisible Body of Christ and the visible species, yet both of them fell into the error of attributing incorruptibilty even to the species.[142] The question arises in connection with the normal reception of the sacrament, and also with profanations of one kind and another. Guitmund and Alger thought it would be humiliating to the Body of Christ to hold that the Eucharist could undergo the same processes as natural food. Consequently they hold that the eucharistic species cannot nourish the body,[143] nor can they be devoured by animals.[144] Alger tries to find support for this view by analyzing the concept of accidental change. Any change or corruption which would seem to befall the consecrated species must be an accidental change, since the sacramental accidents exist in themselves without a subject. But he says that a corruption of accidents is not necessarily involved in an accidental change: a simple alternation may take place in which one accident merely suc-

---

140 *Ibid.*, 809 D-810 A: "Sed quaerunt dialectici, cum substantia panis in corpus Christi conversa, iam non sit panis, in quo fundamento remanent qualitates ut idem qui fuerat panis color et sapor habeant fundari et existere, cum substantia ipsius sacramenti, id est, corpus Christi, nec colore panis sit coloratum, nec sapore sapidum. Ad quod respondendum est quod sicut Deus in omnibus est mirabilis, sic et in istis. Facit enim in suo sacramento accidentales qualitates existere per se, quod in caeteris est impossibile."

141 Cf. Jensen, F., "Eucharistiques (Accidents)'" DTC 5: 1377.

142 Alg., 813 C: "nec solum corpori Christi, sed et ipsi sacramento visibili eadem causa mucorem negamus et putredinem."
Cf. 809 B; Guit., 1445-1447.

143 Guit., 1453 A; Alg., 808, 813 C.

144 Guit., 1448 D.

ceeds the other.[145]   If whiteness is changed into blackness, the whiteness does not corrupt, but simply gives way to the blackness.   An analogous situation is the appearance of the Holy Spirit in the form of a dove, or of fire; as soon as the purpose of the manifestation was achieved, the visible forms simply passed away.   No less exalted conception is to be held of the visible forms which conceal the real presence of the Body of Christ.[146]

Alger does not deny that the species must undergo some change, must pass away, since they are not eternal.[147]   But he holds for what he calls a "simple passing away," so as to protect the species from corruption.[148]   Similarly, both Guitmund and Alger are willing to admit that an apparent corruption of the species takes place.[149]   But this apparent corruption is permitted by God either to stir up faith, or to awaken remorse and repentance in the person responsible for the apparent corruption: perhaps a cleric who in disobedience to ecclesiastical regulation has kept the consecrated species too long.[150]   The consecrated species remain incorrupt even though someone may actually see them apparently being devoured by mice.[151]   If such a thing happens, the species are either taken by the angels to heaven, or they simply disappear.[152]

In taking up this position, Alger and Guitmund ran counter to reason and experience, and their opinion was rejected by subsequent theologians.   Geiselmann suggests that the language of the Humbertian formula prevented Guitmund from arriving at an absolute distinction between the accidents and the sacramental substance.[153]   The same reasoning would hold for Alger.   It is a strange lapse, seeing that both Guitmund and Alger were emphatically correct upon the real point at

---

145 Alg., 809 B: "non fit corruptione secessus, sed sola sui alteratione defectus."

146 *Ibid.*, 809 C.

147 *Ibid.*, 813 C: "Ipsis vero speciebus, cum non sint aeternae, defectum negare possumus."

148 *Ibid.*, "sed ipsum defectum ita dicimus simplicem, ut nullam foeditatis admittamus corruptionem."

149 Alg., 813 D; Guit., 1446 C, 1448 D.

150 Guit., 1448 CD; Alg., 812 A, C.

151 Guit., 1448 D: "Quod si aliquando velut corrosa videantur, responderi potest, id non esse corrosa."

152 *Ibid.;* cf. 1453 A; Alg., 813 B.

153 *Op. cit.*, p. 395.

issue, namely that no corruption of the species, real or apparent, can affect the Body of Christ.[154]   In their formulations of this matter, if they had substituted simple affirmations of the fact for such terms as "seem to be corrupted" and "apparent corruption," they would have expressed the truth clearly and precisely.[155]   This is the one notably weak link in their reasoning; it reveals the immaturity of their philosophy, and points to the need for further development.   But at the same time it should cause no one to overlook the real contributions which Guitmund and Alger made to the development of eucharistic theology.

---

154 Guit., 1449 AB: "Si placet Christo . . . ut haec sacramenta absque sui corruptione a bestiis sive avibus comedi possint: quid hoc ad veritatem, quam credimus, Dominici corporis obstat?"
Cf. 1450 AB; Alg., 811 B, 812 C.

155 Cf. F. Jensen, *loc. cit.*, 1383-1387 for further development of this point. Also St. Thomas, *Summa theologiae*, 3, q. 80, a.3, ad 3.

CHAPTER V:

THE CONTROVERSY CONCERNING THE EUCHARIST AS A SACRAMENT

The central issue in the controversy with Berengar was that of the substantial conversion, and upon this point the positions of the two parties were flatly opposed. Berengar rejected the doctrine of substantial conversion because it was contrary to the evidence of the senses. What is seen upon the altar is bread and wine; but it is impossible that an object should be other than its appearances proclaim it to be; hence bread and wine remain upon the altar. Lanfranc and his successors held on the other hand that through the consecration the bread and wine are marvellously changed into the substance of the Body and Blood of Christ, and that nothing remains of the bread and wine save their unessential qualities, their appearances or accidents.

But, pivotal as this issue was, it did not exhaust the subject matter of the controversy. Instead the question of the substantial conversion was in a cerain sense merely introductory to a further issue and a further controversy. For the Eucharist has not come down through the Christian ages as an absolute and unrelated gift; it has come down as part of the divinely instituted economy of the sacraments. And in the sacraments two elements must be found, that of the visible sign and that of the invisible reality. Any theologian who enters upon a study of the Eucharist must see to it that both of these elements enter genuinely into his system. If a writer approaches the Eucharist from the viewpoint of the visible sign, he must find a reality which is actually and efficaciously produced by means of the visible sign. If another writer stresses the reality, the substantial presence of the Body of the Lord, he must find some place for a genuine Eucharistic symbolism. At the extremes, two solutions must be avoided: a bare symbolism, which would deny all reality to the sacrament, and an exaggerated realism, which would identify the invisible Body with the visible sign.

In this chapter a brief study will be made of the solutions advanced by Berengar and his opponents to meet their respective problems. Berengar, the advocate of symbolism (umbraticus, as Guitmund calls him), must find some reality in the Eucharist, actually produced by the efficacious sign. Lanfranc and his successors, realists (or, in the strong term of Geiselmann, metabolists—*Metabolikers*), must develop a genuine

Eucharistic symbolism. Guitmund of Aversa has summed up the problems of this chapter in one sentence:

> Hic fortasse respondebit umbraticus, quod et dicere solitus est: Si figura est, quomodo veritas? Si sacramentum, quomodo veritas?[1]

Pourrat has devoted a few pages of his *Theology of the Sacraments* to a study of the confusion which was introduced into pre-scholastic sacramental theology by the prevalence of the definition of a sacrament given by St. Isidore of Seville.[2] It is true that St. Isidore reproduced verbally the Augustinian definition of the sacrament as a sign;[3] but in his development of the term, following the etymological procedure which was customary with him, St. Isidore neglected the concept of the sign and considered the sacraments under the aspect of secret, or mystery. "Sacramentum" for Isidore was derived from "secretum"; and Baptism, Confirmation, and Holy Eucharist are sacraments because in them the divine action is concealed under the cover of material elements. This does not mean that Isidore's conception permitted a confusion between the visible sacrament and invisible grace; nor did he fail to realize that the visible rite produces the grace in an efficacious manner. But because the Isidorean definition placed the idea of the sign in the background, there resulted from it a less precise notion of the sacraments.

The authors of the Carolingian period adopted the Isidorean definition unanimously.[4] Its legitimacy was not in question in the Eucharistic controversy of the ninth century, since both Paschasius and Ratramn used it.[5] Hence the weakness of the Isidorean concept did not lie so much in the field of Eucharistic theology as in that of sacramental theology in general: (it was suited indeed to the thing defined, but not exclusively to the thing defined). Following this concept, everything which contains a hidden action of the divinity could be called a sacrament. For Paschasius Radbert, Holy Scripture was a sacrament, be-

---

1 Guit., PL 149: 1457 D.

2 P. Pourrat, *Theology of the Sacraments,* pp. 35-37. Cf. A. Michel, "Sacraments," DTC 14: 525.

3 Isidore, *Etymol.,* lib. 6, cap. 19, n. 39, PL 82: 255 C. "Sacramentum est in aliqua celebratione, cum res gesta ita fit ut aliquid significare intelligatur, quod sancte accipiendum est."

Cf. St. Augustine, *Epist. 55 ad inquisitiones Januarii,* (ed. A. Goldbacher, 1895) CSEL 34: 170.

4 A. Michel, *loc cit.,* col. 527. Raban Maur, *De inst. clericorum,* 1, 24, PL 107: 309. Jonas of Orleans, *De inst. laicali,* 1, 7, PL 106: 134.

5 Radbert, *De corp. et sang. Domini,* PL 120: 1275 A. Ratramn, *De corp. et sang. Domini,* PL 121: 146 C - 147 A.

cause under the letter of the Scriptures the Holy Spirit works efficaciously; and the Incarnation was a sacrament, because in the visible humanity
of Jesus Christ the divinity acts interiorly in secret. In this broad sense
all the mysteries of the Catholic faith might be called sacraments, and
the confusion which resulted could not but impede the development of
sacramental theology. For, as Pourrat writes, "whenever the definition
departed from the idea of sign, it lost something of its precision."[6]

With this background, it seems altogether remarkable that the Beren-
gariaň writers on both sides should have returned with one accord, as it
were, to the Augustinian concept of the sacrament as a sign.

Two definitions prevailed among the writers with whom this study is
concerned. The first is literally of Augustinian origin:

> Sacrificium ergo visibile invisibilis sacrificii sacramentum, id est sacrum
> signum est.[7]

This definition is found in practically identical form in Lanfranc[8] and
Alger.[9] The definition of sacrament as *sacrum signum* does not appear
in Berengar of Tours, although Lanfranc cites from the earlier *opusculum* a definition of identical purport:

> Signacula quidem rerum divinarum sunt visibilia, sed res invisibiles in
> eis honorantur.[10]

The other definition of a sacrament which found widest acceptance
among eleventh and twelfth century writers seems to have originated
with Berengar himself. It is:

> Est enim sacramentum praescribente beato Augustino invisibilis gratiae
> visibilis forma.[11]

Berenger attributes the definition to St. Augustine without specifying
the source. Doubtless it is of Augustinian spirit,[12] but it is not to be
found verbally in St. Augustine's writings, and De Ghellinck holds it to
have been an original expression of Berengar.[13]

---

6 *Op. cit.,* pp. 36-37.
7 St. Augustine, *De civitate Dei,* 10, 5, (ed. E. Hoffman, 1899), CSEL 40: 452.
8 PL 150: 422 D. (Michel, *loc. cit.,* col. 528, improperly cites this as col. 415;
also he wrongly cites Guitmund's definition of sacrament as PL 149: 1147 — it should
be 1475 C.)
9 PL 180: 751 C.
10 Berengar cited by Lanfranc, PL 150: 423 A.
11 D.s.c., p. 114. Cf. pp. 192, 193.
12 See, for example, St. Augustine, *Epist. 98 ad Bonifacium* (ed. A. Goldbacher,
1895) CSEL 34 (2): 521; *Quaestionum in Heptateuchum libri VII* (ed. J. Zycha,
1895) CSEL 28 (2): 305.
13 J. De Ghellinck, S.J., "Une chapître dans l'histoire de la définition des sacrements
au XIIe siècle," Melanges Mandonnet, *Bibliothèque thomiste* 14 (1930), p. 87.

In this definition, the word "forma" should be understood in accordance with Berengar's (and Alger's) usage of the term as "that which falls under the senses, the visible appearance;" and the definition may then be translated, "A sacrament is the visible expression of invisible grace." This Berengarian definition has been traced by De Ghellinick[14] into Ives of Chartres, Alger of Liége,[15] Gratian, Abelard, and Peter Lombard. Doubtless the great success of the definition is due to the Augustinian patronage under which Berengar placed it: it is invariably cited in connection with the genuine definition from the *De civitate Dei,* but with only a general indication of the source: *"Item alibi . . ."* There is no conclusive evidence that Alger of Liége had ever read the *De sacra coena.* It seems therefore that he found the definition in Ives of Chartres, and indeed doubtless it was through the canonical collections of Ives that Berengar's definition entered into the medieval stream.

From this brief sketch of the history of sacramental theology in the pre-scholastic period, it is clear that Berengar and his opponents were in accord at one point, namely in the return to the Augustinian concept of the sacrament as sign. It should not be denied that Berengar himself played a positive part in this development, but it would be exaggerated to claim from him a dominant influence. Rather there seems to have taken place a spontaneous and rapid return to a more worthy concept of sacrament than that of St. Isidore, a development which is all the more surprising in view of the fact that the eleventh century writers had no immediate forerunners upon whom to depend.

But if our authors agreed in their definition of the sacrament, their paths diverged in the development of the idea. Berengar, obsessed with the concept of the sacrament as symbol, attempted to find reality in the Eucharist through a dialectical manipulation of the concepts of conversion and consecration. Lanfranc, Guitmund, and Alger, on the other hand, their faith rooted in the substantial presence, found a genuine and traditional symbolism in the fact that the Lord's real Body, present in the Eucharist and producing great effects in the Eucharist, is present nevertheless and produces these effects *under a sign.*

These considerations open up for study a large area of inquiry, almost every aspect of which is deserving of lengthy special study. Con-

---

14 *Ibid.*
15 PL 180: 751 C.

sequently, a single chapter can do no more than set down the general structure of this theology as it appears in the Berengarian writers, and thus perhaps trace the lines which special study should follow. And again, in accordance with our purpose, the inquiry will be limited to those aspects of the subject in which the theological reasoning of our authors is called particularly into play.

1. *The Pseudo-Realism of Berengar*

The theory of Berengar of Tours concerning the Eucharist as sacrament can be set down in a series of propositions. The Holy Eucharist, after the consecration as before, is bread and wine, not the Body of Christ, but the sign of the Body of Christ. Through consecration, the material elements receive a "conversion," not of their natural being, but of their spiritual significance: they are endowed as symbols with the value of Christ's Body under the aspect of His passion. The effect of the sacrament is the contemplative union of the mind with Christ, the "repose" of the soul in the thought of the Incarnation and Passion. In this section, then, will be developed in turn the Berengarian doctrines of the Eucharistic sign, of the conversion, and of the spiritual reception.

Lanfranc had contrasted the Berengarian and orthodox Eucharistic theology in the following terms:

> You deny the Body and Blood, and place the total reality in the sacrament alone; while we acknowledge the sacrament, and yet faithfully and truly proclaim the reality of the Body and Blood.[16]

Similarly, the Roman profession of faith of 1059 called upon Berengar to renounce all heresy,

> . . . particularly that of which I am accused, which would attempt to establish that the bread and wine which are placed on the altar, after the consecration, are only a sacrament, and not the true Body and Blood of Our Lord Jesus Christ.[17]

Lanfranc's meaning, and Humbert's in the Roman formula, was that Berengar emphasized one truth about the Eucharist to the utter exclusion of the other. The Eucharist *is* a sacrament, *and* it is also the true Body and Blood of Christ. If Berengar rejects the reality of the Body

---

16 Lanf., PL 150: 418 D: "Nam et tu carnem et sanguinem negas, in solo sacramento rem totam constituens; et nos sacramentum fatemur, et tamen utriusque veritatem fideliter ac veraciter confitemur."

17 *Supra*, Ch. iv, n. 43, p. 73.

and Blood, he therefore holds for a bare symbolism, or, in Lanfranc's language, he "places the total reality in the sacrament *alone*."

But Berengar rejected these criticisms as meaningless. There can be no such thing as a "sacrament alone," for the total function of a sacrament is to designate something else—the *res sacramenti*—which is different and distinct from it, and of which it bears the likeness. The term sacrament does not denote a subject, but it says something about an existing thing; it is a designation of relation, or, in the language of Berengar with which we are now familiar, a sacrament is not *ipsum esse*, but *aliquid esse*.[18] Just as the term father is meaningless apart from reference to the child, so *sacramentum* must be considered in relation to the *res sacramenti*—that something be *mere* sacrament, or *solummodo sacramentum*, is unthinkable.

The sacrament exists then only as a visible expression which brings something else to consciousness. Berengar underlines the word consciousness: the sacrament brings the *res sacramenti* to the mind; it does not contain the *res sacramenti* in any realistic manner.[19] The sacraments do not contain the *res*, but rather, through their representative function, put the mind of the receiver in relation to the *res*. Berengar saw in the doctrine of Lanfranc—that the Eucharist should be at once the sacrament of the Body of Christ and the real Body of Christ—a fatal subversion of the concept of the sacrament as sign. But in putting forth this criticism, Berengar assumed that realism identified formally the Eucharistic sign and the reality of the Body and Blood—an unfounded assumption, as we shall see.

Moreover, the sacrament is a *visible* sign, a material being, corporeal, mutable, and temporal, while the Body of Christ, the *res sacramenti*, is invisible, immutable, eternal. It is simply impossible that this material element should be the glorious Body of Christ. Here we see once more the grossly materialistic interpretation which Berengar placed upon the teaching of Lanfranc:

> It must be remembered that according to Augustine the sacrament is something visible, temporal, and mutable. Yet you assert the sacrament to be the Body of Christ — a little portion of His Flesh newly brought into being on the altar. *(Here there is a gap in the text.)* No

18 D.s.c., p. 251. Cf. p. 81 f.
19 Act. Conc. Rom., Martène and Durand, *Thesaurus novus anecdotorum*, 4: 110 B: "aliud in cognitionem venire, non ait in manum, in os, in dentem, sed in cognitionem."

matter how stupid you are, you will not dare to affirm the Body of Christ, either in whole or in part, subject to time or to change.[20]

In his insistence that the *res sacramenti* is not substantially present under the visible sign, Berengar drew an exact parallel between the sacraments of Baptism and Holy Eucharist.[21] Through the consecration which takes place in Baptism, there is effected a change of the baptismal elements into the death and resurrection of Christ, not in their real actuality, but in a symbol. And just as there is in Baptism no presence of the actual death of Christ, neither is there the presence of the actual Blood of Christ in the Eucharist.[22]

Thus Berengar insisted upon the sacrament as sign, its visibility and transiency, its relative character. But the Body of Christ is the absolute, the *res sacramenti,* spiritual and invisible. It cannot be in heaven and earth at the same time. The *res sacramenti,* therefore, is not on the altar; and what is seen upon the altar is bread.

But Berengar emphatically denied he held "bread alone" to exist upon the altar. The sacrament is bread, yes, but not bread alone.[23] It is at this second point of the Eucharistic theology that realistic language begins to appear in the writings of Berengar. We have already seen how ready he was to affirm that after the consecration the true Body and Blood of Christ are present on the altar; even that the bread and wine are changed, or converted, into the true Body and Blood of Christ.[24] Now we must inquire into the precise nature of this Berengarian "conversion."

For Berengar, the conversion which takes place in the Eucharist is brought about by consecration, the principle which constitutes the sacrament in being. But in his analysis of the concept of consecration, he argues in a fashion quite similar to his discussion of the nature of a sacrament. To consecrate does not mean to cause a being to exist, but to

---

20 D.s.c., p. 114: ". . . quod sacramentum attendi oportet auctore Augustino esse visibile, temporale, mutabile aliquid. Corpus enim Christi, cuius sacramentum esse asseris portiunculam recens factam in altari tibi ipsi contrarius, . . . nulla vecordia tempore obnoxium mutabileque esse vel pro parte vel pro toto affirmare audebis."

21 *Ibid.,* p. 128: "De sacramento regenerationis pervenit (Ambrosius) ad tractandum de sacramento refectionis per omnia comparabile." Cf. pp. 128, 156, 151-2.

22 Berengar cited by Lanfranc, PL 150: 439 A: "Non est autem vera Christi mors in baptismo. Igitur nec verus eius sanguis in hoc sacramento." Cf. D.s.c., pp. 150, 155, 157.

23 D.s.c., p. 207: "non nego panem esse, sed affirmo non solum."

24 *Supra,* p. 75.

act upon a being which is already in existence; it is a transitive action, and presupposes a being as its subject:

> Consecration, or the action of consecrating is not a subject, but it is in a subject.[25]

And, in an argument precisely the same as that with which he criticized Humbertian formula,[26] he concludes that the consecrated object must remain after the consecration.[27] If bread and wine receive a consecration, bread and wine continue to exist; and after the consecration bread and wine are on the altar.

And yet through this consecration there takes place a "conversion" of the bread and wine into the Body and Blood of Christ. Berengar attempts to resolve the apparent contradiction by playing again upon the meaning of a word, this time the term "conversio." He says that conversion is not an univocal concept, but is subject to many qualifications.[28] Not every conversion is such as to result in the destruction of one subject and the coming into existence of another. When God said, "Ad vos convertar," He did not say that His essence would cease to exist, but He merely announced a change of His position with regard to the Hebrew people. If Saul becomes Paul, there does not take place a cessation of one human nature and the coming into being of another, but simply a change in his relation to God. In these examples of conversion, there is neither a *corruptio subiecti* nor a *generatio subiecti*.[29]

And the conversion which takes place in the Eucharist is of a similar kind. It is not a physical change, but a spiritual conversion:

> According to nature, that which you see with bodily eyes is bread; but considering the divine blessing, that bread is the Body of Christ, after which you must strive with the eyes of your soul, the eyes of faith.[30]

The effect of consecration, the term of the conversion, is that the bread

---

25 D.s.c., p. 210: "consecratio vel consecrari subiectum non est, sed in subiecto." Cf. pp. 188, 217.

26 *Supra*, p. 74: ". . . non poterit constare omnis affirmatio parte subruta."

27 D.s.c., p. 216: "Nec convincere poteris adesse consecrationem, ubi consecratum auferes." Cf. p. 91.

28 *Supra*, p. 75, nn. 55, 56.

29 D.s.c., p. 146: "Nulla in his secundum corruptio, nulla secundum subiectum generatio." Cf. p. 145.

30 *Ibid.*, p. 177: "Quantum ad naturam, panis est, quod tu vides oculis corporis; quantum ad divinam benedictionem, ipse panis est corpus Christi, quod attendere debes oculis cordis, oculis fidei."

and wine become sacraments. "The bread consecrated on the altar is a sacrament."[31] And Berengar is willing to venerate as the Body of Christ this material bread become a sacrament through consecration.[32] The bread and wine indeed *are* the Body and Blood of Christ, but only because they are sacraments[33]—that is, signs of the Body and Blood.

The real meaning of consecration and conversion, then, is that the bread and wine, remaining what they were in their material being, acquire a new value, that of the Body of Christ. By means of the consecration, the elements possess a higher meaning, a superior worth. Before the consecration, the bread and wine were mere material elements, devoid of religious significance; through consecration they acquire the value of a means of salvation.[34]

Here we are at the center of Berengar's theory of the Eucharist as sacrament. Through consecration, the material elements, are "carried to a higher plane;"[35] before consecration "the bread and wine possessed no efficacy for eternal life; after consecration they have that efficacy."[36] Berengar draws an analogy from the Incarnation of the Word:

> The Word made Flesh assumed what it was not without ceasing to be what it was. Similarly, the bread consecrated on the altar loses its profaneness, its inefficacy, but not its proper nature; and it acquires as it were in place of that nature a divinely increased dignity and worth.[37]

And to this spiritual conversion there corresponds a purely spiritual reception of the Eucharist. We do not receive the actual Body of Christ in Holy Communion; we receive only material bread and wine. The

---

31 *Ibid.*, p. 68: ". . . panis in altari consecratus est sacramentum."

32 *Ibid.*, p. 34: "sensualem panem consecratione altaris factum sacramentum esse profiteor corpus Christi."

33 *Ibid.*, p. 143: ". . . corpus et sanguinem, quia sacramenta."

34 Macdonald, *Berengar and the Reform of Sacramental Doctrine*, p. 321: "Through the mystery of the consecration a change takes place in the effectiveness of the elements, and through this operation they become a sacrament, the pledge of salvation and the medium of spiritual life. The consecrated or sacramental bread and wine have a religious value."

35 D.s.c., p. 116: ". . . in melius provehi." Cf. *Acta Conc. Rom.*, Martène and Durand, *op. cit.*, 4: 107 A, C; Lanf., PL 150: 419 C: D.s.c., pp. 98, 109, 141, 156, 163, 165, 179, 279.

36 *Ibid.*, p. 145: "Inefficax erat panis natura ante consecrationem ad vitam aeternam, post consecrationem efficax."

37 *Ibid.*, pp. 98-99: "Denique verbum caro factum assumpsit, quod non erat, non amittens, quod erat, et panis consecratus in altari amisit vilitatem, amisit inefficaciam, non amisit naturae proprietatem, cui naturae quasi loco, quasi fundamento dignitas divinitus augeretur et efficacia."

real efficacy of the sacrament is to operate "in thought," in the contemplation of the believer.[38] Through the physical reception of the bread and wine, made a symbol of Christ crucified through consecration, the thought of the believer is borne towards Christ and is absorbed in Him. And the effect of this contemplation is to provide the faithful person with the strongest motive to imitate the virtues of Christ and to regulate his life according to the example of the crucified Savior:

> "Through the physical eating and drinking of the material elements, you recall to mind the spiritual eating and drinking of the Flesh and Blood of Christ which takes place in the soul. While you refresh yourself interiorly upon the thought of the Incarnation of the Word and His Passion, you ought also order your interior life with the same humility as that with which the Word became Flesh, and with His patience in the shedding of His Blood. How you ought to excel in patience, and be absorbed in these things, and find joy in them, just as in physical food and drink your body finds repose.[39]

By way of a critical summary, it may be remarked first that the subjective character of Berengar's sacramental theology is manifest. His system does not permit the passage of an objective gift from God to the receiver, whether that gift be considered as the reception of the Body of Christ or of grace through the sacrament. The believer finds for *himself* refreshment and repose in the thought of the Incarnation and Passion;[40]

---

38 *Ibid.*, p. 287: ". . . praesta ut . . . cogitatione sumamus . . . corpus tuum." p. 157: "Ad cordis devotionem, ad cordis contuitum necessario te trahit (b. Ambrosius), ubi venientes ad accipienda sacramenta altaris adoratur."

39 *Ibid.*, p. 223: ". . . ut per comestionem et bibitionem corporalem, quae fit per res exteriores, per panem et vinum, commonefacias te spiritualis comestionis et bibitionis, quae fit in mente, de Christi carne et sanguine, dum te reficis, in interiori tuo incarnatione verbi et passione. ut secundum humilitatem per quam verbum caro factum est et secundum patientiam per quam sanguinem fudit interioris tui vitam instituas, quanta debes emineas patientia ut in eis tibi adquiescas, in eis tibi adgaudeas, sicut in exteriori tuo, in cibis tibi et potibus, adquiescis."

Cf. pp. 148, 157, 237, 238, 250, 255, 274; Lanf. PL 150: 440 C.

Cf. also Zwingli, *Illustrissimis Germaniae Princip. in Conciliis Aug. Congreg.*, p. 546 (cited by Möhler, J. A., *Symbolism*, ed. 5, tr. by J. B. Robertson, London, 1906, p. 250): "Quo factum est ut veteres dixerint corpus Christi vere esset in coena; id autem . . . cum propter istam . . . certam fidei contemplationem, quae Christum ipsum in cruce propter nos deficientem nihil minus praesentem videt, quam Stephanus carnalibus oculis ad dexteram Patris regnantem videret. Et adseverare audeo, hanc Stephano revelationem et exhibitionem sensibiliter esse factam, ut nobis exemplum esset, fidelibus, cum pro se paterentur eo semper modo fore, non sensibiliter, sed contemplatione et solatio fidei."

The similarity is striking between the Berengarian doctrine and that of the 16th century Swiss reformer, whose Eucharistic symbolism became almost standard in Protestant theology.

40 D.s.c., p. 255: "Reficiendo se, acquiscendo sibi in incarnatione et passione verbi."

thus the sacramental realization in its entirety begins and ends within the religious consciousness of the believer. This is not a doctrine of the application to the recipient of the merits of Christ through the direct efficacy of the visible sacrament; but rather the visible sacrament is a means of stimulation for the mind, to awaken in it the remembrance of the Incarnation and Passion of Christ.[41]

Thus the "conversion" of which Berengar writes is exclusively in the moral order, and affects not the sacramental elements, but the sentiments of the believer with relation to the elements. The analogies of moral conversion which Berengar himself used to describe his concepts of conversion—that of God turning towards His people and of Saul becoming Paul—are therefore apt descriptions of his theology, a system in which the traditional doctrine of the sacrament as efficacious symbol plays no part.[42]

Finally, Berengar's subjective Eucharistic theology, along with his insistence on a total parity between Holy Eucharist and Baptism, raise certain questions concerning his attitude towards the sacraments *in communi*, and even towards the fundamental doctrines of revealed Christianity in general. It has been mentioned in the course of this study that contemporaries of Berengar attributed to him errors in other fields than that of Eucharistic theology, but that we have no proof of this for lack of documentation. Yet the assertion of Theoduin of Liége, repeated by Guitmund of Aversa, that Berengar denied the efficacy of infant baptism, is entirely consistent with his Eucharistic theology.[43] For Berengar, there is no passage of an objective gift in the Eucharist; the total efficacy of the sacrament depends upon the contemplation of the recipient. Yet he insists that Baptism and the Eucharist are wholly on a par. Hence it would seem he might hold the baptism of infants ineffectual, since they are incapable of contemplation. And even further, Berengar's insistence on the moral element of the Eucharist, on its value only as a graphic representation of the Passion of Christ for the contem-

---

41 Cappuyns, M., "Bérenger de Tours," DHGE 8: 403-4: "Il s'agit moins de ce que la théologie postérieure à appellé une application des merites du Christ que d'une sorte de suggestion bienfaisante, par le moyen de symboles, de ce que le Christ est pour nous et nous engage à être, dans son incarnation et sa passion."

42 Harnack, *op. cit.*, p. 49, has had considerable difficulty with the Berengarian concept of conversion. He writes: "Yet the tropical view . . . was not equivalent for Berengar to the symbolical. . . . A 'conversio' takes place; but for Berengar this expression has certainly an unusual sense," etc. And in note 5 on the same page: "It must be assumed that it [i.e. the 'conversio'] rests on an accommodation; for although there answers to the sacrament a *res sacramenti*, which is created by the consecration, yet it is certainly not a question of transmutation," etc.

43 Theoduin, *Ad Henricum regem contra Brunonem et Berengarium*, PL 146:

plation of the recipient, throws some doubt on his orthodoxy concerning the objective character of revealed Christianity in general. Indeed, Geiselmann goes so far as to assert that, not only for the Eucharist, but also for the Incarnation and the redeeming Passion themselves, Berengar acknowledged not a real, but only a moral, or "didactic" meaning.[44] The heresy of Berengar emphasizes once more the striking truth that the mysteries of Christianity are not a collection of disparate articles but an integrated pattern, and the denial of one is likely to cause the subversion of the whole.

2. *Orthodox Symbolism*

Any discussion of Eucharistic symbolism among the opponents of Berengar must be rooted in the same thought which guided them, the thought of the substantial conversion. The Body of Christ is actually and substantially in the Eucharist, and the presence is achieved through substantial conversion. But the further fact is that the Body of Christ is also present under a sign, under appearances not its own, in a signifying mystery. Consequently, it is not simply heretical to say that the Body of Christ is present "in figure," if the term figure be applied to the visible sign and not to the substance of the Body and Blood of Christ. The idea which the Council of Trent later condemned was that of a presence *simply*—"tantummodo"—in figure, in such a way as to exclude the reality of the substance.

A Catholic discussion of the sacrament, must, therefore, take account of both elements, the reality and the figure. In this final section, we shall see how this was done by Lanfranc, Guitmund and Alger. We shall study their sacramental doctrine in three stages: first, a work of analysis, of sharp division between the visible sign and the invisible substance; second, a work of synthesis, of the bringing together of the visible sign and the invisible substance, not to confuse them, but to show that the effects of the Eucharist are attributable not to the visible sign but to the Body of Christ under the sign; third, the effects of the Eucharist, the object and work of Christ in this sacrament. This threefold development corresponds to the medieval distinction, still current, in which the Holy Eucharist is studied under the aspect of *sacramentum tantum,* of *sacramentum-et-res,* and of *res tantum.* Our study will emphasize

---

44 *Op. cit.,* p. 352: "Erkennt doch Berengar der Menscherwerdung und dem Erlösungsleiden nicht dingliche, sondern nur didaktische Bedeutung zu."
1429 A. Cf. Vernet, *loc. cit.,* col. 727.

the *ratio signi,* since it is in this that orthodox symbolism in its active sense is found; and will merely indicate our authors' treatment of the third, the *ratio significati,* since under this aspect are comprised great Eucharistic truths which deserve and are receiving much special study.

Every discussion of the personal controversy between Lanfranc and Berengar must begin with the Roman formula of 1059. We have seen that the language of this formula gave Berengar what he considered one of his most conclusive arguments against the substantial conversion.[45] Again, in the preceding section of this chapter, we saw that the term "solummodo sacramentum" of that formula provided the point of departure for Berengar's exposition of his own sacramental doctrine.[46] But now, even at the risk of wearisome repetition, we must go over the same ground once more, since this formula—or rather Berengar's misquotation of it—gave Lanfranc the opportunity to express his own view of the Eucharist as sacrament.

In describing the condemned teaching of Berengar, the Roman formula made use of the expression, "solummodo sacramentum et non verum corpus et sanguinem."[47] But when Berengar himself cited the formula, in the earlier *opusculum* of which we have only quotations in Lanfranc's treatise, he inserted the word "solummodo" to modify "verum corpus et sanguinem" as well as "sacramentum." So that in Berengar's citation the formula read, "solummodo sacramentum et non SOLUMMODO verum corpus et sanguinem." The effect of Berengar's introduction of this single word was to set up an absolute opposition between the sacrament and the Body and Blood, so as to make the affirmation of the one involve necessarily the denial of the other. If this Berengarian dichotomy could be sustained, then he would be right in attributing to Humbert, to Lanfranc, and to his Catholic opponents in general a doctrine of exaggerated realism.

But Lanfranc emphatically rejected the dilemma thrust upon him by Berengar. In the early chapters of his treatise he asserts repeatedly that Berengar had done nothing more than set up a straw man. The Church does not hold to the reality of the Body and Blood in such a way as to deny the sacrament; the term "solummodo corpus et sanguinem" did not appear in the formula at all:

---

45 *Supra,* pp. 73-74.

46 *Supra,* p. 103.

47 See once more, the language of the formula, cited, p. 73.

The other expressions [Humbert] used, but the adverb *solummodo* he did not place there at all. Hence whatever in your lying way you attempt to conclude or infer from that word . . . totally breaks down.[48]

Lanfranc then sets down in broad and sweeping terms the Catholic doctrine of the Eucharist as sacrament. In this expression we see a valuable preliminary sketch and outline of the entire subject presently under discussion, similar in its scope and importance to Lanfranc's profession of faith in the substantial conversion. We see in it also a correct phrasing of the *status questionis* as it existed between himself and Berengar:

> The first proposition, in which it is said: "the bread and wine of the altar are only sacraments," is your opinion and that of your disciples. But the latter proposition, which states, "the bread and wine of the altar are only the true Body and Blood of Christ," is no one's opinion. For the Church of Christ believes that the bread is changed into Flesh, and the wine into Blood, in such wise as also to acknowledge the Eucharist to be a sacrament, of the Lord's Passion, of the divine propitiation, of peace and unity, and finally of the Body and Blood taken from the Virgin. But each of these significations is achieved in its own distinct way.[49]

The Eucharist, then, is not only reality but also sacrament. And Lanfranc specifies that he accepts the term "sacrament" in the Augustinian sense which is acceptable to Berengar: the sacrament is a sign.[50] As sign, it signifies not one thing only, but a variety of things, and these various significations are not identical: in other words, Lanfranc states in general terms that the Eucharist is not a commemorative sign of the Passion in exactly the same way that it is a demonstrative sign of peace and unity among Christians. Within this general framework is contained the entire teaching of the anti-Berengarian writers concerning the significance of the Eucharist as sacrament.

---

48 PL 150: 419 B: "Caetera namque dixit, adverbium *solummodo* nequaquam posuit. Quidquid igitur ex mendacio te mendaciter astruente colligitur, quidquid infertur, necessario totum dispargitur, infirmatur, cassatur."
Cf. 416 B, 417 BC, 418 D.

49 *Ibid.*, 415 A: "Prior quidem sententia, per quam dicitur: Panis et vinum altaris solummodo sacramenta sunt, tua est, tuorumque sequacium. Posterior vero quae enuntiat: Panis et vinum altaris solummodo sunt verum Christi corpus et sanguis, nullius hominum est. Nam . . . Ecclesia Christi, sic panem in carnem, vinum credit converti in sanguinem, ut tamen salubriter credat et veraciter recognoscat sacramentum esse Dominicae passionis, divinae propitiationis, concordiae et unitatis, postremo assumptae de Virgine carnis ac sanguinis singula suis distinctisque modis. . . ."
Cf. 416 C, 418 D.

50 *Ibid.*, 422 C: "Et nos sacramentum, de quo agimus, sacrum esse signum credimus, et credendum suademus."

In attempting to analyze more closely the elements that enter into the sacrament, Lanfranc adopts the distinction which had already been used by Berengar:

> The sacrifice of the Church is made up of *(confici)* two elements, . . . the visible appearance of the species, and the invisible Flesh and Blood of Our Lord Jesus Christ, the *sacramentum* and the *res-sacramenti* — and the *res* (to use your very words) is the Body of Christ.[51]

Berengar also had used the term "sacrament" to designate the visible species, and Body of Christ to denote the invisible *res*. But for Berengar the visible sacrament merely signified the invisible *res*, which was in heaven and not on the altar. While in Lanfranc's view, both elements are actually present in a mysterious manner in the Host, which is at the same time the sacrament signifying the *res* and the *res* itself.

Alger of Liége discusses more fully than Lanfranc the Eucharistic sacrament as a sign. The procedure of Alger is to set forth points of similarity between the Eucharist and other sacraments; then to contrast the Eucharist with other sacraments both of the Old Law and of the New; and finally to distinguish sharply within the Eucharist itself, the visible sign from the invisible reality.

Like other sacraments the Eucharist is a sign.[52] Like other sacraments the Eucharist is a transient gift which is meant to endure only during the present life.[53] The sacrament of the altar has been instituted to show forth the death of the Lord only until He comes, because then, when we shall see Him face to face, there will be no further need of mysteries.[54] It is in this sense of the temporal character of the sacrament that Alger interprets the meaning of the Post-Communion for Ember Saturday in September:

> Perficiant in nobis, Domine, quaesumus, tua sacramenta quod continent, ut quae nunc species gerimus, rerum veritate capiamus.

---

51 *Ibid.*, 421 BC: ". . . sacrificium scilicet Ecclesiae duobus confici, duobus constare, visibili elementorum specie, et invisibili Domini nostri Jesu Christi carne et sanguine, sacramento et res sacramenti; quae res (ut verbis tuis utar) est corpus Christi."

52 Alg., PL 180: 716 D: "Constat ipsum sacramentum sicut caetera esse significativum."

53 *Ibid.*, 762 C: "Nec solum comparatur sacramentum corporis Christi caeteris sacramentis consignificando, sed et in corpore Christi aeternaliter non permanendo . . . non in corpore Christi manere perpetualiter, sed post hanc vitam omnino desinere creditur, sicut et caetera sacramenta."

54 *Ibid.*, 746 A: "Quia ergo hoc sacramentum non est in aeternum mors Christi annuntianda, sed tantum donec veniat, quia postea nullis mysteriis egebimus, constat illud transitorium esse signum et temporale, quo tantum egemus nunc, dum videmus per speculum et in aenigmate."

Alger takes the "veritas" of this prayer as meaning the total manifestation of the truth. We possess the "veritas" of the Body and Blood even during this life, but we have it under the shadow of the sacramental appearances. At the end of time we shall possess the same "veritas," in manifest vision, face to face.[55]

If the Eucharist is like other sacraments in its character of impermanence, it is unlike them in other respects. The manna of the Old Law and the Eucharist of the New are alike in that which they signify, namely, Christ,

> . . . but the sacrament of the bread signifies Christ more intimately than the manna, since the manna signified Christ to come, while the bread signifies Him actually present. The manna signified Christ only in an external way, while the bread is substantially converted into the Body of Christ, and thus formally signifies the Body of Christ.[56]

The sacraments of the Old Law merely foreshadowed in figure the reality which was to come; in the New Law is given the reality along with the figure; and in the glorious future life we shall have the reality unveiled. The Old Testament promised the reality but did not give it. The New Testament gives the reality, but does not manifest it. The future life will manifest the same reality in intuitive vision.[57]

Alger further distinguishes the sacrament of the Eucharist from the other sacraments of the New Law. In so far as their material being is concerned, the other sacraments are figures only; their natures are not changed so as to become what they signify. The water of Baptism and the oil of confirmation remain what they were: they signify the Holy Spirit, but they do not contain Him essentially; they possess Him in figure and in power. And Alger continues:

> Only the sacrament of the bread and wine is so changed as substantially to cease to be what it was before; its substance becomes the Body of Christ; its external appearance, however, remains, and signifies the Body of Christ and contains it.[58]

---

55 *Ibid.*, 762 D: "Frustra oraremus, ut quod nunc specie geritur, rerum veritate capiamus, si ibi etiam hujus sacramenti haberemus umbram, ubi facie ad faciem sicut est videre speramus Christi gloriam."

Similarly Lanf., PL 150: 435 B. Cf. Guitmund's different interpretation of the prayer, PL 149: 1468, and de la Taille, *Mysterium Fidei*, p. 486.

56 *Ibid.*, 762 AB: "Cum tamen sacramentum panis familiarius significet Christum quam manna, quia manna futurum, panis praesentem, manna tantum extrinsecus, panis ita ut substantialiter sit conversus in corpus Christi, et formaliter significet corpus Christi."

57 *Ibid.*, 763 AB.

58 *Ibid.*, 761 A: "Solum sacramentum panis et vini ita mutatur ut substantialiter non sit quod ante fuerat; sed substantia ejus corpus Christi fiat, forma vero remanens ipsum significet et contineat."

Having thus laid down the preliminary distinctions, Alger then proceeds to give his analysis of the Eucharistic sacrament:

> The form of bread and wine and the other qualities remaining —
> these alone can truly be called *sacramentum*. The invisible substance,
> however, which is contained under this sacrament, and into which the
> substance of bread and wine is changed — this can truly be called, and
> it is, the Body of Christ.[59]

Like Lanfranc, then, Alger distinguishes two elements in the Eucharist,
the *sacramentum tantum,* which is the species of bread and wine as informed by consecration, and the invisible substance of the Body and
Blood of Christ.

But much more emphatically than Lanfranc, Alger insists on the real
distinction between the visible *sacramentum* and the invisible Body of
Christ. They are not *unum et idem,* but *aliud et aliud.*[60] Alger holds
that it is far from the Catholic position to identify the transient species
of bread and wine with the substance of the changeless Body of
Christ.[61]   And if sometimes the species are *called* the Body of Christ,
this must be understood as a figurative and not a true predication.[62]

Here Alger, to refute the Berengarian charge of exaggerated realism,
is employing a sharp scholastic distinction between the species, taken precisely as species ("praecisive," in the scholastic term) and the Body and
Blood of Christ which they signify and contain. He uses this distinction to explain a difficulty which Berengar had drawn from the letter of
St. Augustine to Boniface. If Augustine says in that letter that the
sacrament of the Body and Blood *is* the Body and Blood "secundum
quemdam modum," he is referring to the visible form and appearance of
the elements—which indeed are not the Body and Blood of Christ, except figuratively and by a certain likeness. But the substance which

---

59 *Ibid.,* 752 C: "Formam panis et vini et caeteras elementorum remanentes et visibiles qualitates, sacramentum tantummodo vere dici et esse: substantiam autem illam invisibilem, quae ipso sacramento operta est, et in quam panis et vini substantia translata est, vere et proprie dici et esse corpus Christi testatur Augustinus."

60 *Ibid.,* 752 D: "Quae ergo duo esse approbat, visibile sacramentum et invisibilem rem sacramenti, non *unum et idem,* sed *aliud et aliud* esse demonstrat."

61 *Ibid.,* 753 C: "Absit ergo ut transitoria species panis et vin, sit vera substantia vel vera species immutabilis Christi."

62 *Ibid.:* "Sed si aliquando dicitur corpus Christi, nuncupative et non vere oportet intelligi."

these species contain, and into which the substance of bread and wine is changed, is truly and properly the Body of Christ.[63]

Again, Alger insists that these two elements do not enter into composition with one another, but remain distinct. The failure to make this distinction is responsible for the error of the impanationists, who, through an improper use of terms and analogies, try to bring the *sacramentum* and the *res sacramenti* into composition.[64] It is one thing to say that the Body of Christ is both reality and figure. It is another to say that man is a body and soul. There is a grammatical similarity between these two expressons, but they are utterly unlike in meaning.[65] Body and soul enter into composition to form one human nature; but the accidents of bread in this sacrament are not part of the Body, nor are they accidents of the Body—they are only the sign of the Body.

To sum up the teaching of Lanfranc and Alger at this first stage of the inquiry, it is clear that they distinguish between two elements in the sacrament, really distinct, the *sacramentum tantum,* which is the visible species of bread and wine remaining after the consecration, and the *res sacramenti,* which is the invisible substance of the Body of Christ. There is no confusion or composition between these two elements; the *sacramentum* is not the Body of Christ, and the Body of Christ is not the *sacramentum;* but the Body of Christ is the invisible *res,* and the species are its sign.

With this background and this emphatic distinction in our minds, we are at first sight startled to see Lanfranc, and Guitmund and Alger after him, assert that the Body of Christ in the Eucharist is itself a sacrament and a sign.[66] In their attribution to the actual Body of Christ of a truly

---

63 *Ibid.,* 753 D: "In quo notandum est sacramentum corporis Christi, secundum quemdam modum, id est, similitudinarie et nuncupative, non proprie corpus Christi vocari, quantum ad elementorum speciem et formam: quod tamen vere et proprie corpus Christi vocatur et creditur, quantum ad substantiam quam continet in et in quam panis et vini substantia conversa est."

64 *Ibid.,* 754 C: ". . . ex indifferenti et impropria usurpatione nominum vel similitudinum . . . de sacramento et re sacramenti ita loquuntur, ut prave intelligentibus, quasi in unum quid accipiantur."

65 *Ibid.,* "Sed cum dicitur, 'corpus Christi est veritas et figura,' numquid pro una persona accipiendum est, sicut cum dicitur, 'homo est corpus et anima?' Similis quidem est grammatica sed non similis intelligentia."

66 Lanf., PL 150: 424 C: "Christus ergo Christi est sacramentum."
Guit., PL 149: 1458 A: "Cum sit verum Christi corpus, dicatur et signum."
Alg., PL 180: 792 D: "Verum corpus Christi invisibile . . . sit sacramentum visibilis corporis Christi."

sacramental function we believe we find their principal contribution to the study of the Eucharist as sacrament, and the heart and center of an orthodox Eucharistic symbolism: the doctrine, namely, of the real Body of Christ as *sacramentum-et-res* in the economy of this sacrament. None of them uses the actual term, and none of them seems to have grasped the full significance of the idea; consequently we must leave for the moment the simple examination of their texts and attempt to interpret the ideas which must have led them to call the actual Body of Christ the *sacramentum* of itself.

From all that we have seen so far, it might appear that Lanfranc and Alger are in agreement with Berengar in assigning a distinction of two elements in the Eucharist, both really distinct: the *sacramentum,* or the sensible sign, and the invisible *res sacramenti,* or the Body of Christ. But of course they explained these two terms differently. Lanfranc and Alger placed both of the sacramental elements in actual connection with the consecrated species: after the consecration, the substance of Christ's Body and Blood is actually present under the species in much the same way as the substance of bread and wine was actually present under them before the consecration—with the exception, of course, that the accidents of bread and wine do not inhere in the Body and Blood of Christ as formerly they did in the bread and wine, but by the divine power are miraculously sustained in themselves. But as we have seen, Berengar placed no such actual connection. For Berengar, there is between the consecrated species and the *res sacramenti* no more than a moral connection: through the consecrated species one is reminded of the immolated Savior; one contemplates His sufferings, becomes absorbed in the thought of them, and determines henceforth to regulate his life with a similar humility and patience.

Thus, in brief, for Berengar, the sensible sign is bread, and the *res sacramenti* is not on the altar but is in heaven only. While for Lanfranc and Alger, the sensible sign is not bread, but the accidents of bread, and the *res sacramenti* is actually made present on the altar through the consecratory words. The event of the real presence does not induce any change in Christ, but only in the bread through the substantial conversion. And in the permanent sacrament the actual Body of Christ remains present as long as the species themselves remain in being. *With regard to the consecrated species,* therefore, the Body of Christ is the *res,* and the species themselves are its *sacramentum,* or sign.

But even as distinguished from the Berengarian view, it is apparent that the distinction of the sacrament into two elements—*sacramentum* and *res sacramenti*—is not sufficient to express the entire richness of the Eucharistic symbolism. For this distinction would make the significative power of the sacrament end in the designation of Christ's presence on the altar. But to bring about Christ's presence on the altar is not the end of the sacramental process. *The end of that process must be to produce some effect in us who receive.* In the opening paragraphs of this section, we cited Lanfranc saying that the Eucharist as sacrament is significant of many things—of the Lord's Passion, of the divine propitiation, of concord and unity—in addition to the effect merely of bringing about the real presence on the altar. Consequently, the Body of Christ existing on the altar cannot be called simply the *res sacramenti;* but the significance of the sacrament must be thrown forward, as it were, so as to signify effects which are produced in us, the actual destinaries of the sacrament. If, as Lanfranc says, concord and unity among Christians are signified by this sacrament, then concord and unity must be the *res sacramenti,* or at least must enter into the *res sacramenti.*

Moreover, if certain great effects are produced in us through the sacrament, these effects must be attributed to the Body of Christ as their cause, and not merely to our participation in the *sacramentum tantum* as sharply distinguished from the Body of Christ. For the *sacramentum tantum,* even as informed by the words of consecration, is only the accidents of bread and wine, and these accidents are efficacious only by reason of the underlying substance of the Body and Blood of Christ, which they signify and contain. The accidents of bread and wine are not a life-giving sacrament, but the Body and Blood of Christ, signified and contained under these transient species, are the bread of eternal life.

And finally, if the *res sacramenti* is something produced in us, and does not merely terminate in the substantial conversion; and if the production of the *res sacramenti* must be attributed to the Body of Christ as its cause; then it must be attributed to the sacrament also, because Christ in the Eucharist does not act on our souls absolutely, but only in connection with the sacrament itself.

For all these reasons, therefore, it becomes clear that the division of the sacrament into *sacramentum tantum* and *res sacramenti* (Body of Christ) in insufficient. The Body of Christ itself must enter into the internal economy of the sacrament. The Body of Christ must in fact *be* the sacrament, producing its effect in us. With regard to the consecratory action, the Body of Christ is *res.* But with regard to us the Body of Christ under the visible species is *sacramentum.*

If these principles are kept in mind, it may be easier to understand the somewhat startling assertion of Lanfranc that the "Body of Christ in the Eucharist is a sacrament of itself." We believe we see in this statement of Lanfranc an imperfect foreshadowing of a doctrine which was to receive rich development in later medieval writers, and which is an important element in Catholic Eucharistic theology today: the doctrine, namely, of the Body of Christ as *sacramentum-et-res* in the Eucharist.[67]

In their scientific treatment of the Eucharist, medieval theologians inserted between the two elements *sacramentum tantum* and *res tantum,* a third element, which is *sacramentum-et-res,* the true Body of Christ under the sacramental species. This middle element is totally lacking in Berengar's theology, and its presence in Lanfranc, Guitmund, and Alger is, we think, the key to the controversy concerning the Eucharist as sacrament. The stumbling-block for Berengar was his inability to understand how the sacrament could be at one and the same time symbol and reality, and to save the symbol he abandoned the reality. But here in the doctrine of the *sacramentum-et-res,* are both elements. The Body of Christ in the Eucharist is the reality, because its presence is assured through the substantial conversion. But the Body of Christ is sacrament, and therefore sign, because it is present under a sensible sign, under appearances not its own. And the Body of Christ it is that under these appearances produces the great effects that are summed up in the term *res tantum.* Thus the Eucharistic Body of Christ may be called the sacrament of the Body of Christ, not so as to relate the Eucharistic Body merely to the historical Body, but to the whole Christ, the Mystical Body, since the final end and product of the sacrament is to bring about the incorporation of the faithful in Christ. The Body of Christ in the Eucharist is the sacrament of His Mystical Body, which is the Church. Here is an efficacious symbolism surpassing even that of Baptism: a participation of the believer in Christ, not only in His power, but in the very reality of His divine Person, under the symbolic elements.

We believe this doctrine is found actually, if not in the literal terms

---

67 The doctrine of the *sacramentum-et-res* is clearly taught in Hugh of St. Victor, *De sacramentis Christianae fidei,* 2, 8, PL 176: 466-467. Cf. *Summa sententiarum,* 6, 3, PL 176: 140. M. de la Taille, *Mysterium Fidei,* pp. 507-510, traces development from Lanfranc through Guitmund, Alger, William of St. Thierry, Innocent III, and Thomas Waldensis. For modern importance of *sacramentum-et-res* doctrine, see L. Billot, *De Sacramentis Ecclesiae,* ed. 6, vol. I, pp. 105-115, 321. Cf. also H. De Lubac, *Corpus Mysticum, L'Eucharistie et L'Église au Moyen Age,* Paris (Aubier), 1944, pp. 83-84, 118, 128.

themselves, in Lanfranc's insistence that Christ is the sacrament of Himself:

> The sacrament of the Body of Christ is His Flesh, which we receive in the sacrament, concealed under the appearance of bread; and His Blood which we drink under the appearance and taste of wine. The Flesh is the sacrament of the Flesh, and the Blood is the sacrament of the Blood.[68]

More surprisingly still, Lanfranc asserts that the invisible Body of Christ in the Eucharist is the sign of the visible and palpable Body.

> By the invisible, intelligible, spiritual Flesh and Blood, is signified the visible and palpable Body, manifestly full of grace and divine Majesty.[69]

The immediate objection to this doctrine is that an invisible thing cannot be a sign of a visible thing.[70] Lanfranc answers this objection correctly by relating the significative power of the Body of Christ to the visible species: *"sacramentum corporis Christi . . . caro ejus est, quam* FORMA PANIS OPERTAM *. . . accipimus."* The Body of Christ in the Eucharist is indeed invisible, but it is somehow made visible through its connection with the species, and can thus fulfill the function of a sign.[71]

But when Lanfranc applies the signifying power of the Body of Christ to a *res,* or thing signified, he relates it back to the natural, historical ("corpus visible, palpabile") Body of Christ immolated:

> When the Body is broken, and is distributed for the salvation of the people; and when the Blood is poured from the chalice and received into the mouths of the faithful, His death on the Cross, and the shedding of the Blood from His side, are symbolized.[72]

---

68 PL 150: 423 D: "Sacramentum corporis Christi . . . caro ejus est, quam forma panis opertam, in sacramento accipimus, et sanguis ejus quem sub vini specie ac sapore potamus. Caro videlicet carnis, et sanguis sacramentum est sanguinis."

69 *Ibid.,* 424 A: "Carne et sanguine, utroque invisibili, intelligibili, spirituali, significatur Redemptoris corpus visibile, palpabile, manifeste plenum gratia et divina majestate."

70 See this objection made to Lanfranc's teaching by Gerhoch of Reichersberg, cited in de la Taille, *op cit.,* p. 507.

71 Billot, *op.cit.,* p. 115, note "Sacramentum-et-res est sensibile solum *per accidens,* ratione scilicet sacramenti exterioris cum quo nexum habet necessarium atque infallibilem. . . ." Cf. De la Taille, *op. cit.,* p. 510.

72 Lanf., 424 A: "Quorum alterum quidem dum frangitur, et in populi salutem dividitur; alterum vero effusum de calice ab ore fidelium sumitur, mors ejus in cruce, et sanguinis ejus de latere emanatio figuratur."

Now it is true indeed that the Eucharist is the commemorative sign of Christ in His passion and death—that is the sacrifice of the Mass; and it is true that the Sacrifice of the Cross, which finds its mystical prolongation in the Mass, is the radical source and cause of all the effects which the Eucharist produces in those who participate in it. But the full value of the concept of Christ's Body as *sacramentum-et-res* has not been expressed until its significance has been thrown forward to embrace us who share in the actual life of Christ through the sacrament. Thus Lanfranc's approach is only partial and imperfect, and Alger of Liége simply repeats Lanfranc.[73] For a richer development we must go to Guitmund of Aversa.

Guitmund begins by agreeing with Lanfranc that it is no obstacle to our faith to hold that the Body of Christ in the Eucharist is both sacrament and reality.[74] He says that Scripture refers to Christ, even in His historical existence, as a sign, *signum cui contradicteur*.[75] In the Eucharist, then, He is the *Sign of Salvation*,[76] which is the fruit of the Redemption applied to us.[77] The glorified Christ in heaven now in His Humanity and Divinity is the *Sign of the Eternal Covenant* between God and man.[78] And in the Eucharist, He is the Sign of the *Peace* which we enjoy as sharing in the covenant.[79] Finally, His natural Body born of Mary was the *Sign of His Mystical Body*, which is the Church.[80] And in the Eucharist, He is the Sign of that same Mystical Body, incorporating us as members of Christ our Head,

> for as often as we receive it, we show ourselves to be Christians, that is, spiritually reborn. Consequently, we declare ourselves crucified with Christ, and dead with Him, and buried with Him through Baptism unto death — but also we declare that we have risen with Him![81]

---

73 PL 180: 792 A, C, D.

74 Guit., PL 149: 1457 C, 1458 A, 1460 CD.

75 *Ibid.*, 1457 D: "Non legistis in Evangelio ipsum Christum signum appellari, . . . signum cui contradictur?"

76 *Ibid.*, 1458 B: "Simile quoque ratione cibum altaris Domini . . . ejusdem salutis nostrae credimus significativum."

77 *Ibid.*, 1458 A: "Christus enim, quoniam seipsum pro nobis obtulit, factum est nobis signum redemptionis."

78 *Ibid.*, "Christus denique inter Deum et homines mediator . . . signum est foederis sempiterni."

79 *Ibid.*, 1458 C: ". . . hujus tam saluberrimae pacis, sacrosancta altaris oblatio a . . . signum cui contradicetur?"

80 *Ibid.*, 1459 BD: ". . . ipsum suum proprium, quod de beata Virgine sumpserat corpus, corporis sui, quod est Ecclesia, signum est, et figura et sacramentum."

81 *Ibid.*: ". . . quia quotiescumque id sumimus, nos utique Christianos esse, id est, spiritualiter natos ostendimus. Consequenter ergo et concrucifixos, et conmortuos et consepultos Domino nostro, per baptismum in mortem, sed et consurrexisse nos declaramus.'

In this beautiful analogy in three stages we see unfolded some of the riches of the Catholic Eucharistic symbolism.   The Holy Eucharist is the continuation of the Incarnation and Redemption; through this sacrament are actually applied to our souls the benefits which the Incarnate Redeemer won for the world in objective fashion on the Cross.   This is not a bare symbolism, as it was for Berengar, a mere memorial of Christ and an inducement to imitate His virtues.   The actual presence of Christ in the sacrament is the guarantee of the reality of our hopes.   When we participate in His Body under the sacramental appearances, we actually share His life, as Guitmund points out, and enter in a most real and intimate fashion into the mysteries of His Passion, and Death, and Resurrection.

This presentation seems to us to explain the insistence of Lanfranc, Guitmund and Alger that the Body of Christ in the Eucharist is a sacrament of itself.   We may then conclude this section on the Body of Christ as *sacramentum-et-res* with Guitmund's analysis of the internal economy of our sacrament:

> Wherever the Eucharist is called the sacrament of the Body of Christ, or wherever similar language is used, we so interpret it: the Eucharist is the sacrament which is the Body of the Lord, so as to be truly His Body, and sacrament of other things, namely of the further benefits of which we have been speaking.[82]

We will close our study of orthodox Eucharistic symbolism with a brief survey of the "benefits" of which Guitmund has been speaking, the *res sacramenti,* a term which designates the final end and object of Christ's work in His sacrament.

The *res sacramenti* may be viewed as multiple or as one.   We have seen Lanfranc's assertion that the Eucharist is the sign of many things: of the Lord's Passion, of the divine propitiation, of peace and unity.   But in fact, all these benefits are adequately summed up in one formula: the sacrament of the Eucharist is the sign of the union of the faithful with Christ, as members with their Head, of their participation in His divine life, and their sharing in His Mysteries.   The technical term, "grace," as effect of the Eucharist is seldom   found   in   the   anti-Berengarian

---

82 *Ibid.,* 1460 B: "Ubi sane invenitur eucharistia dici sacramentum corporis Domini, aut constructionem verborum, sic resolvimus: Eucharistia est sacramentum quod est corpus Domini, ut ipsa quidem sit vere corpus Domini, sacramentum vero sit aliarum rerum, praedictorum videlicet bonorum."

writers,[83] but they speak often of eternal life, of salvation, of union with Christ; and in reality these terms are synonymous. For the grace of the Christian life is union with Christ, which is eternal life possessed even in the present time, and the source and principle of salvation. The multiplicity of the *res sacrament* is found in the fact that the grace of union is signified by this sacrament in various ways. It is signified in its *cause*: and thus the Eucharist is the sign of the Lord's Passion; in its *present actuality*, and the Eucharist is the sign of the union of the faithful with Christ and His Church; and in its *future splendor*, and the Eucharist is the pledge of eternal life and the guarantee of the glorious resurrection of the Body. This manifold significance of the Eucharist is clearly found in our writers; here we shall indicate their teaching along general lines, and cite references for further inquiry into this vast subject.

The Holy Eucharist is the sign of the Passion of Christ. This, of course, is the Sacrifice of the Mass. It should surprise no one to find that the early medieval writers assign no special treatment to the Eucharist precisely as a sacrifice. For them it was patent that the Body of Christ is possessed now by the Church under the aspect of His death; the *sacramentum* was the sacrifice, and the sacrifice was real because the presence of the immolated Christ under the sacramental appearances was real.[84] Here the doctrine of the *sacramentum-et-res* is extremely important: the Body of Christ is offered up in reality because it is present in reality, but it is offered up symbolically, because it is present under a sign.

The teachings of Lanfranc, Guitmund and Alger on the Eucharistic sacrifice are a valuable part of that great medieval tradition which modern writers, such as Billot, Vonier, and Masure have done so much to restore. A passage from Alger will illustrate their basic doctrine:

> It is to be noted that our daily sacrifice is said to be the same as that which Christ offered once upon the Cross, if we consider it from the point of view of the same true substance of the Body of Christ, on the Cross and upon the altar. But our daily sacrifice is called also a representation of His sacrifice, that is, a figure or an expression. This does not constitute an essentially different Christ in the Mass and on the Cross, but simply shows that the same Christ who was once immolated

---

83 But see Alg., PL 180: 751 A, 774 A.

84 A. Vonier, *Sketches and Studies in Theology*, London, (Burns, Oates, and Washbourne), 1940, pp. 80, 83.
Cf. C. V. Héris, *Le mystère du Christ*, Paris, (Desclée), 1928, p. 338.

and offered upon the Cross, is daily immolated and offered upon the altar, but in a different manner. There He was offered in the reality of the Passion in which He was slain for us; here He is offered in the figure and image of His Passion. Christ does not really suffer again in the Mass; but the memory of His Passion is daily kept by us.[85]

The Eucharist is the sign of our union with Christ and His Church. This is the present effect of the Eucharist, the effect which is produced in the souls of those who receive. Repeatedly our authors use the language of Christ in John 6 as proof that the reception of the Body of Christ actually produces in us union with Christ and our abiding in Him.[86] Alger of Liége adds the valuable observation that our union with Christ in this sacrament is achieved primarily with His sacred Humanity, but that through the humanity we become partakers of the divinity and sharers of the divine nature.[87] Both Lanfranc and Alger stress the two-fold reception of the Eucharist, *in ore* and *in corde*. One is as necessary as the other.[88] If the spiritual reception is said to be more important than the corporal, this does not mean that the Christ we receive into our souls is different from the Christ of the Eucharistic communion; but only that the spiritual reception is always productive of grace, while the corporeal reception may fail to produce grace because of the evil disposi-tions of the communicant.[89] And finally, the sacrament is only pro-ductive if it results in a union of charity and love among the members of the Mystical Body of Christ. For in this sacrament we are united

---

85 Alg., PL 180: 786 D: "Notandum ergo quia quotidianum nostrum sacrificium idem ipsum dicit cum eo, quo Christus semel oblatus est in cruce, quantum ad eamdem veram hic et ibi corporis Christi substantiam: quod vero nostrum quotidianum illius semel oblati dicit esse exemplum, id est figuram vel formam; non dicit ut hic vel ibi essentialiter alium Christum constituat, sed ut eumdem in cruce semel, in altari quotidie alio modo immolari et offeri ostendat; ibi in veritate passionis qua pro nobis occisus est hic in figura et imitatione passionis ipsius, qua Christus non iterum vere patitur, sed ipsius vere memoriae memoria passionis quotidie nobis iteratur."

On the Sacrifice of the Mass, see Lanf., PL 150: 423-425; Guit., PL 149: 1455; Alg., PL 180: 786, 795-796.

86 Lanf., 425 D, 427 D, 429 A; Guit., 1492 AB; Alg., 769 D, 770 D, 772 D, 774.

87 774 D: ". . . incorporat, sicut corporis et animae Dominicae, sic etiam ipsius divinitatis suae. . . ."

Cf. M. J. Scheeben, *The Mysteries of Christianity*, (tr. by C. Vollert, S.J.), St. Louis (Herder), 1946, p. 526.

88 Lanf., 425 CD: "Utraque comestio necessaria, utraque fructuosa. Altera indiget alterius, ut boni aliquid operetur."

89 Alg., 773 D, 774 A, cf. 749 D - 750 A.

On union with Christ as effect of this sacrament, see Lanf., 425, 427 D, 429 BC; Guit., 1492; Alg., 749-751, 769-774, 794.

with Christ in His capacity of Head, and the union with the Head necessarily includes a union with the other members.[90]

And at last, the Eucharist is the sign of the glorious resurrection of the Body, and of eternal life. Alger writes that although the Eucharist is primarily spiritual food, yet it profits the body also. And he cites the promise of the Savior that he who eats this food will not be defrauded of eternal life, but Christ will raise him up in the last day.[91] Thus the faithful person is united to Christ in all the Mysteries of His life, not only the sorrowful Mysteries of the Passion, but also the glorious Mysteries of His Resurrection and Ascension: and the Eucharist is the proof that He has really loved us *in finem*. Finally, it is worthy of note that Alger requires the moral element of a pure and holy life in those who participate in the Eucharist; not in Berengar's sense of the moral element as the chief benefit of the Eucharist, but in that of a good disposition on the part of those who receive:

> Thus it is certain that with Him and through Him we shall obtain a like glory of dignity in eternal life, if with Him and through Him we strive to preserve a like grace of innocence in this life.[92]

---

90 On the unity of the Mystical Body, cf. Lanf., 425; Guit., 1459-1461; Alg., 749, 794.

91 774 B: "Quod autem ad corpus attinet, nec ei vita aeterna fraudetur, sed in resurrectione mortuorum in novissimo die."

92 747 D: "Certumque esset, hoc pacto nos cum ipso per ipsum, in vita aeterna, similem dignitatis obtinere gloriam, si cum ipso per ipsum, in hac vita similem innocentiae servare voluerimus gratiam . . . maxime cum ipse moriturus . . . vitae aeternae pactum nobis assignaverit, et ipse a mortuis resurgendo, in se capite nostro, quomodo corpus suum glorificare deberet ostenderit."

GENERAL CONCLUSIONS AND SUMMARY

Although theological controversies generally bear on particular doctrines of faith or morals, yet invariably broader problems and more fundamental oppositions underlie the special questions at issue. Very often the events and movements of secular history will exert profound influence even in the realm of theology. For example, the rise of the Protestant heresy in northern Europe coincided with a growing spirit of nationalism which resulted from the discoveries of new continents and the expansion of national trade. Again, the intellectual spirit and temper of an age will influence its theology. Nineteenth-century rationalism and modernism grew out of the thought that the progress of natural science had rendered obsolete any system of supernatural and revealed religion. At the bottom of every heresy there is the idea, either expressed or implied, that human science and supernatural mystery are unalterably opposed, and heresy will issue either in the flat rejection of the mystery or the attempt to give it a purely rational explanation.

Needless to say, the influence of extraneous factors becomes crucial, and an apparent conflict between faith and reason is experienced, only among heterodox theologians. Only a theology which is exclusively man-made needs to be cut to fit the latest development of natural science or secular history. Over it all and through it all, the perennial theology is richly present in the world, making steady progress, but at peace and undisturbed because it has been founded upon changeless principles revealed by God.

But the fact remains that it is impossible to understand any theological controversy apart from the historical and intellectual context in which it had its place.

The context of the Berengarian controversy was the pre-scholastic period, extending from the ninth century to the twelfth, a period of transition between the conservatism of the post-patristic age and the great expansion of scholasticism which took place in the twelfth and thirteenth centuries. The pre-scholastic scholars had at their disposal two sources of knowledge, Holy Scripture and the tradition of the Fathers, and a gradual but sporadic stream of Aristotelian dialectics—not the metaphysics—which came to them principally through the translations and commentaries of Boethius. Scholastic theology was born of the union between Reason and Authority which took place in the pre-scholastic period. The pre-scholastic writers had patristic authority for their conviction that the two sources did not conflict, but could be harmonized into one cohesive body of knowledge. Authority was of primary importance, of course: nothing must be taught except what had been revealed by God in Scripture and tradition, and proposed for belief by the teaching authority of the Catholic Church. But reason had its lawful *role*, ancillary, auxiliary, and propaedeutic, for the better understanding and expression of revealed doctrine.

It was possible, however, in the confusion which necessarily accompanied the early stages of this theological science, for a writer to exaggerate the *role* of reason and apply the principles and methods of an immature philosophy even against the stream of traditional authority. And Berengar of Tours, eleventh-century *scholasticus* of Tours and arch-deacon of Angers, a man of blameless life but of bold and independent spirit, delighted with dialectics, stands as the ablest of the anti-authoritarian dialectical school. Berengar attempted to explain the Eucharist, the Mystery of Faith, wholly in the light of the principles of the philosophy which he had learned, rejected tradition and the teaching of the Church, and fell inevitably into heresy.

The heresy of Berengar of Tours is cumulative: it begins on the deep level of the principles of theological knowledge, and expresses itself in his theory of the Eucharist.

In the first place, then, Berengar built on reason, not on faith. It is true that he paid lip-service to traditional teaching, and attempted to square his doctrine with it, but he emphatically proclaimed the "incomparable superiority" of reason to traditional authority as a source of religious knowledge. And when the *magisterium* was brought to bear upon his teaching, he renounced the Church altogether and rejected its authority.

And further, the "reason" upon which he built consisted in an immature philosophical system, the dialectics of the schools. Berengar simply did not know metaphysics, and yet his basic Eucharistic error was in the metaphysical order. His was a sensist metaphysics, the belief that the proper object of sensible experience is being in its totality, that the senses grasp not only the appearances of an object but also its essence, in a direct and immediate manner. Thus, the distinction between substance and accident was lost on him, and he was led to regard as absurd a doctrine which held for a change of substance while the accidents remained. His inability to understand the traditional teaching of a real presence of Christ's Body and Blood *in specie aliena* led him to adopt a crude and materialistic interpretation of the doctrine of substantial conversion; and his dialectical criticism of the formulas of realism (his argument that "if bread is called the Body of Christ, then bread must remain") is mere logic-chopping and a playing with words.

But Berengar had to take account of the realistic language of the Fathers, and thus built up a positive theory of the Eucharist as mere sign and symbol. Through the consecration there takes place a conversion, not of the Eucharistic elements themselves, but of the sentiment of the believer with respect to them. The elements remain what they had been before, but they become the Body and Blood of Christ in the contemplation of the recipient, and are endowed for him with the value of Christ's passion and death. Thus the conversion is purely in the moral order, and the Eucharistic activity begins and ends within the consciousness of the believer himself. The subjective character of Berengar's Eucharistic theology renders suspect his sacramental theology in general, since the idea of the efficacious symbol is excluded; and his sensist metaphysics throws some doubt upon the orthodoxy of his belief in supernatural religion. If nothing exists save that which can be grasped by the senses, then mysteries and their revelation are impossible.

The philosophy of the opponents of Berengar was no more mature than his. They accepted the doctrine of substantial conversion, not because their reason made it evident, but because the doctrine was contained in Scripture and tradition, and was taught by the Church and believed by the faithful. No more can be said today. The real distinction between substance and accident does not prove the Catholic doctrine of the Eucharist, but it effectually prevents any adversary from proving in a conclusive manner that it contains a contradiction in terms. The Mystery of Faith remains.

But the exercise of dialectics enabled the adversaries of Berengar to clarify and organize the revealed teaching, and carry it to a point of development considerably in advance of the Fathers and post-patristic writers. In the first place, they teach that the doctrine of substantial conversion does not involve creation nor local movement, but a simple change of the substance of bread and wine into the substance of Christ's Body and Blood. Thus they distinguish two modes of being of Christ's Body, the natural mode, in which His Body is in heaven in glorious immortality at the right hand of the Father; and the sacramental mode, in which He is present in many places on earth. And the presence of Christ on earth does not involve change on His part since the change is altogether on the part of the bread.

And further, against the capharnaitic interpretation of Berengar, they teach that since the presence of Christ's Body is not bound by the dimensions of the bread, the presence of Christ in the Eucharist is not a partial but a total presence. Christ is whole and entire in the Host and in every particle; moreover, in the doctrine of concommitance as introduced by Alger, His living Body is present under the appearance of wine, and His living Blood under the appearance of bread. The two-fold consecration does not affect the totality of Christ's presence, bu is done in imitation of the Savior's practice at the Last Supper, and for the sake of the significance of the Passion.

Although the substance of bread and wine is changed into the substance of Body and Blood, yet the accidents of bread retain a real and not phantasmal existence in their proper character as accidents. And Alger of Liége adds the important clarification that the accidents after the consecration do not inhere in any substance but by the divine omnipotence are miraculously sustained in themselves.

And finally, the Catholic opponents of Berengar effectively conclude the series of pre-scholastic discussions of the *veritas* and the *figura,* by saying that there is in this sacrament both the reality and the symbol: the reality, because Christ's Body is actually present, the symbol, because He is present under the sign of bread and wine. Thus the Holy Eucharist is the true Body and Blood of Christ; but as sacrament, under the sacramental symbols, it is the sign of many things, of the Lord's passion, of the union of the faithful with Christ, and of the unity of the Mystical Body, the bond of love which should unite all those who partake of the one heavenly bread.

But the importance of the Berengarian controversy cannot be confined merely to the field of Eucharistic theology. It had a great bearing on the development of scholasticism and the scholastic method. During this controversy much was done to clarify the relative competencies of the two sources of knowledge, reason and authority. The dialectical excesses of Berengar were inimical to the development of theology, since they might have aroused anti-intellectual reaction and a suspicion of rational inquiry of any kind. But it is simply providential that his errors evoked replies from men as skillful in dialectics as himself who were at the same time men of faith, Catholics, and first-rate theologians. It is true to say that the Berengarian controversy provided a bridge between the monographic literature of the pre-scholastic period and the great theological syntheses which were soon to make their first appearance.

BIBLIOGRAPHY

(Under "Sources and Works, General" are cited those which concern the cultural, philosophical, and theological background of the pre-scholastic period. Under "Sources and Works, Special" are cited those which concern matters particularly involved in our study of the later period of the Berengarian controversy.)

List of Abbreviations

CSEL: *Corpus scriptorum ecclesiasticorum latinorum*, Vienna, 1866 ff.

DB: Denziger, H., Bannwart, C., Umberg, J., *Enchiridion symbolorum definitionum et declarationum*, edd. 21-23, Freiburg-im-Breisgau, 1937.

DHGE: Baudrillart, etc., *Dictionnaire d'histoire et de géographie écclesiastique*, Paris, 1912 ff.

DTC: Vacant, Mangenot, *Dictionnaire de théologie catholique*, Paris, 1909 ff.

MGH: Pertz, Mommsen, etc., *Monumenta Germaniae Historica*, Hanover, 1826 ff.

PL: Migne, *Patrologiae cursus completus, series latina*, 221 vols., Paris, 1844-1864.

Sources, General

Alcuin, *Adversus Elipandum*, PL 101: 231-300.

————*Adversus Felicem*, PL 101: 119-230.

————*De dialectica*, PL 101: 949-976.

————*Epistola 83 ad Carolum Magnum*, PL 100: 269-274.

————*Epistola ad Fredegisum*, PL 101: 57-64.

————*De grammatica*, PL 101: 349-902.

Ambrose, St., *De mysteriis*, (ed. Quasten) *Florilegium Patristicum*, Fasc. VII, Pars 3a, Bonn, (Hanstein), 1936.

————*De sacramentis, Ibid.*

Anastasius, *Epistola ad Giraldum abbatem, de veritate corporis et sanguinis Christi Domini*, PL 149: 432-436.

Ascelin, *Epistola ad Berengarium*, PL 150: 66.

Augustine, St., *De civitate Dei* (ed. E. Hoffmann, 1900), CSEL 40, I-II.

————*De doctrina Christiana*, III, PL 34: 15-122.

————*De fide et symbolo*, (ed. Zycha, 1900), CSEL 41: 3-32.

————*De ordine*, II, (ed. Knoll, 1922), CSEL 63: 121-185.

————*Epist. 98 ad Bonifacium*, (ed. Goldbacher), CSEL 34 (2): 520-533.

————*Epist. 120 ad Consentium, De trinitate*, (ed. Goldbacher), CSEL 34: 704-722.

————*In Joannis Evangelium*, PL 35: 1379-1976.

————*Quaestiones in Heptateuchum, libri septem*, (ed. Zycha, 1895), CSEL 28 (2): 3-506.

————*De scriptura sacra Speculum*, (ed. Weihrich, 1899), CSEL 12: 3-385.

————*De symbolo, sermo ad catechumenos*, PL 40: 627-668.

Boethius, *De differentiis topicis, libri quattuor*, PL 64: 473-1216.

————*In categorias Aristotelis, libri quattuor*, PL 64: 159-294.

————*In Isagogen Porphyrii Commentorum*, (ed. Brandt), CSEL 48 (1906).

————*In librum Aristotelis de interpretatione, libri sex, editio secunda*, PL 64: 393-640.

————*Quomodo substantiae in eo quod sunt, bonae sint*, PL 64: 1311-14.

————*Quomodo Trinitas unus Deus ac non tres dii*, PL 64: 1247-1256.

Cassiodorus, *De artibus ac disciplinis liberalium litterarum*, PL 70: 1149-1220.

————*De institutione divinarum litterarum*, PL 70: 1105-1150.

————*Epistola XLV Boetio viro illustri patricio Theodoricus rex*, PL 69: 539-541.

Charlemagne, *Capitula de doctrina clericorum*, MGH (Legum) 1: 107.

————*Encyclica de litteris colendis*, MGH (Legum) 1: 52.

Conc. *Francofordiensis epistola synodica, ad praesules Hispaniae missa*, PL 101: 1331-1346.

Durand of Troarn, *Liber de corpore et sanguine Christi contra Berengarium et ejus sectatores*, PL 149: 1375-1424.

Florus, *Sermo de praedestinatione*, PL 119: 95-102.

Fredegisus, *De nihilo et tenebris*, PL 105: 751-756.

(Gerbert), *De corpore et sanguine Domini*, PL 139: 179-188.

Hugh of Langres, *Tractatus de corpore et sanguine Domini contra Berengarium*, PL 142: 1321-1331.

Hugh of St. Victor, *De sacramentis christianae fidei*, 2, 8, PL 176: 461-472.

Isidore, St. *Etymologiarum, lib. II, De rhetorica et dialectica*, PL 82: 123-154.

John the Scot, *Commentarius in s. Evangelium secundum Joannem*, PL 122: 297-348.

————*De divisione naturae*, PL 122:441-1022.

————*De praedestinatione liber*, PL 122: 347-440.

Jonas of Orleans, *De cultu imaginum*, PL 106: 307-388.

Manegold, *Opusculum contra Wolfelmum Coloniensem*, PL 155: 149-176.

Martianus Capella, *De nuptiis philologiae et mercurii, libri IX*, (ed. A. Dick) Leipzig (Teubner) 1925.

Othloh, *Dialogus de tribus quaestionibus, Prologus*, PL 146: 59-134.

Paschasius Radbertus, *Liber de corpore et sanguine Domini*, PL 120: 1255-1350.

Peter Damian, St., *Epistola XIII, ad capellanos Gothifredi ducis*, PL 144: 358-367.

————*Opusculum Tricesimum Sextum, De divina omnipotentia in reparatione corruptae, et factis infectis reddendis*, PL 145: 595-622.

Prudentius of Troyes, *De praedestinatione contra Joannem Scotum Erigenam*, PL 115: 1009-1336.

Rabanus Maurus, *De clericorum institutione libri tres*, PL 107: 397-398.

Ratherius, *Epistola I ad Patricium, De corpore et sanguine Domini*, PL 136: 643-648.

Ratramnus of Corbie, *De corpore et sanguine Domini*, PL 121: 103-170.

Servatus Lupus, *Epistola CXXVIII ad dominum regem*, PL 119: 601-605.

Sigebert of Gembloux, *Liber de scriptoribus ecclesiasticis*, PL 160: 547-592.

Summa sententiarum, 6, 3, PL 176: 137-154.

Theoduin of Liége, *Ad Henriecum regem contra Brunonem et Berengarium epistola, De corpore et sanguine Domini*, PL 146: 1439-1442.

Wolphelm of Brauweiler, *Epistola de sacramento Eucharistiae contra errores Berengarii*, PL 154: 414.

Sources, Special

Alger, *De sacramentis corporis et sanguinis Dominici*, Sanctorum Patrum Opuscula Selecta, 23, (ed. H. Hurter, S.J.), Innsbruck, 1873.

————*De sacramentis corporis et sanguinis Dominici*, (ed. J. B. Malou), Louvain, 1847, PL 180: 739-854.

————*De sacrificio Missae*, Sanctorum Patrum Opuscula Selecta, 23, (ed. H. Hurter, S.J.), Innsbruck, 1873.

————*De sacrificio Missae*, (ed. J. B. Malou), Louvain, 1847, PL 180: 853-856.

Berengar, *De sacra coena adversus Lanfrancum liber posterior*, (edd. A. F. and F. Th. Vischer), Berlin, 1834.

Guitmund, *De corporis et sanguinis Christi veritate in Eucharistia, libri tres*, Sanctorum Patrum Opuscula Selecta, 38, (ed. H. Hurter, S.J.), Innsbruck, 1879.

————*De corporis et sanguinis Christi veritate in Eucharistia, libri tres*, PL 149: 1427-1494.

Lanfranc, *De corpore et sanguine Domini adversus Berengarium Turonensem*, PL 150: 407-442.

————*In b. Pauli Epist. Comment.*, *Epist. ad Corinth. prima*, PL 150: 155-215.

Martène, E., and Durand, U., *Thesaurus novus anecdotorum*, t. 4, Paris, 1717.

Works, General

Bach, J., *Die Dogmengeschichte des Mittelalters*, Vienna, 1874.

Barrett, H. M., *Boethius, Some Aspects of His Times and Work*, Cambridge, 1940.

Brunhes, G., *La foi chretienne et la philosophie, au temps de la Rénaissance Carolingienne*, Paris, (Gabriel Beauchesne) 1903.

Butler, C., O.S.B., "Monasticism," *The Cambridge Medieval History*, I, (edd. H. M. Gwatkin, M. A., and J. P. Whitney, B.D.), New York, 1911.

Cappuyns, M. O.S.B., "Boèce," DHGE, 9 (1937) 348-380.

————*Jean Scot Erigène, sa vie, son oeuvre, sa pensée*, Louvain (Abbaye du Mont César), Paris (Desclée de Brouwer), 1933.

Cambridge Medieval History (H. M. Gwatkin and J. P. Whitney, edd.), Vol. 1, New York, 1911.

Cayré, F., *Précis de Patrologie*, 2 vols., Paris, (Desclée), 1930.

Chesterton, G. K., *Orthodoxy*, New York, (Dodd, Mead and Co.), 1941.

Chollet, A., "Aristotelisme de la scholastique," *DTC*, 1: 1869-1887.

Clerval, A., *Les Écoles de Chartres au moyen-âge*, Paris, 1895.

Collins, J., "Progress and Problems in the Reassessment of Boethius," *The Modern Schoolman*, 23 (1945) 1-23.

Dawson, C., *The Making of Europe*, New York, (Sheed and Ward), 1934.

————*Medieval Religion and Other Essays*, New York, (Sheed and Ward), 1934.

De Ghellinck, J., S.J., "Dialectique, théologie, et dogme au Xe - XIIe siècles," *Beiträge zur Geschichte der Philosophie des Mittelalters*, Festgabe Zum 60. Geburtstag Clemens Baümker, Münster, (Supplement band), 1913, 79-99.

————*Litterature latine au moyen-âge*, Bibliothèque Catholique des sciences religieuses, Paris, 1939.

————*Le mouvement théologique du XIIe siècle, Études, recherches et documents*, Paris (Gabalda), 1914.

————"Réminiscences de la dialectique de Marius Victorinus dans les conflits du XIe et du XII siècle," *Revue néo-scholastique*, 18 (1911) 432-435.

De Wulf, M., *History of Medieval Philosophy*, I, 3rd Engl. Ed. trans. from 6th French Ed., E. Messenger, London (Longmans, Green and Co.), 1935.

Diefenbach, *Glossarium latino-Germanicum, mediae et infimae aetatis*, Frankfort-on-Main, 1857.

Duckett, E., *Gateway to the Middle Ages*, New York, (Macmillan), 1938.

Endres, J. A., "Studien zur Geschichte der Frühscholastik," *Philosophisches Jahrbuch*, 26 (1913) 160-169.

Ernont, A., Meillet, A., *Dictionnaire étymologique de la langue latine*, Paris, 1932.

Faivre, E., *La question de l'autorité au moyen-âge*, Paris, 1890.

Gilson, E., *Reason and Revelation in the Middle Ages*, New York, 1938.

Grabmann, M., *Die Geschichte der Scholastischen Methode*, I, Freiburg-im-Breisgau, 1909.

Haskins, C., *The Renaissance of the Twelfth Century*, Cambridge, U. S., 1933.

———*The Rise of Universities*, Brown University, the Colver Lectures, New York (Henry Holt Co.), 1923.

Haureau, B., *Histoire de la philosophie scholastique*, Paris, 1872.

Heitz, Th., *Essai historique sur les rapports entre la philosophie et la foi, de Bérenger de Tours à D. Thomas d'Aquin*, Paris, 1909.

Laistner, M. L. W., *Thought and Letters in Western Europe*, New York, (The Dial Press), 1931.

Mandonnet, P., *Siger de Brabant et l'avérroisme latin au XIIIe siècle*, Collectanea Friburgensia, Fasc. VIII, Fribourg (Suisse), 1899.

Macdonald, A. J., *Authority and Reason in the Early Middle Ages*, Oxford, (University Press), 1933.

McSorley, J., C.S.P., *An Outline History of the Church by Centuries*, 4th rev. ed., St. Louis, (Herder), 1945.

Mignon, A., *Les origines de la scholastique et Hughes de Saint-Victor*, I, Paris, 1895.

Newman, J. H., *Historical Sketches*, II, New Impression, London, (Longmans, Green, and Co.), 1903.

Otten, B., S.J., *A Manual of the History of Dogmas*, II, St. Louis, (B. Herder), 1918.

Paré, J., Brunet, A., Tremblay, P., *La Rénaissance du XIIe siècle, les écoles et l'enseignement*, Refonte complète de l'ouvrage de G. Robert (1909), Paris (Libr. Philosophique J. Vrin), Ottawa (Inst. d'Études médiévales), 1933.

Patch, H. R., *The Tradition of Boethius*, New York, (Oxford University Press), 1935.

Peltier, H., "Radbert Paschase," *DTC*, 132 (1937), 1628-1639.

Perrone, J., *Praelectiones* Theologicae, I, Ed. 36, Ratisbon, 1881.

Pirenne, H., *Histoire de Belgique*, I, 5th Ed., Brussels, 1929.

Poole, R. L., *Illustrations of the History of Medieval Thought and Learning*, 2nd Ed., Revised, London, 1920.

Prantl, C., *Geschichte der Logik in Abendlande*, II, Leipzig, 1861.

Rand, E. K., *Founders of the Middle Ages*, Cambridge, U. S., 1928.

Reuter, H., *Geschichte der religiösen Aufklärung in Mittelalter*, 2 vols., Berlin, 1875-1877.

Rousselot, X., *Études sur la philosophie dans le moyen-âge*, I, Paris, 1840.

Sartiaux, F., *Foi et science au moyen-âge*, Paris, 1926.

Thesaurus linguae latinae, (Teubner), 1900, vol. V part 2.

Thompson, J. W., *The Medieval Library*, Chicago, (University of Chicago Press), 1939.

Tixeront, J., *History of Dogmas*, Trans. from the 5th French Edition by H. L. B., vol. III, The End of the Patristic Age, St. Louis, 1916.

Van de Vyver, A., "Les étapes du dévelopment philosophique de haut moyen-âge," *Revue belge de philologie et d'histoire*, 8 (1929) 432-452.

Whitney, J. P., *Hildebrandine Essays*, Cambridge Univ. Press, 1932.

Works, Special

Batiffol, P., *Études d'histoire et de théologie positive*, ser. 2, (6th edition), Paris, 1920.

Billot, L., *De ecclesiae sacramentis*, I, Ed. VIa Romae, 1924.

Brigué, L., *Alger de Liége, un théologien de l'eucharistie au debut du XIIe siècle*, Thèse pour le doctorat en théologie, Paris, (J. Gabalda), 1936.

Brillant, M. (ed.), *Eucharistia, encyclopédie populaire sur l'eucharistie*, Paris, 1934.

Cappuyns, M., O.S.B., Review of work of L. Brigué, *Bulletin de théologie ançienne et médiévale*, 3 (1937-1940), No. 748.

———"Bérenger de Tours," *DHGE*, 8 (1934), 385-407.

Chollet, J. A., *La doctrine de l'eucharistie chez les scholastiques*, Paris, 1908.

Coghlan, D., *De sanctissima Eucharistia*, Dublin, 1913.

De Crozals, J., *Lanfranc, archevêque de Cantorbéry, sa vie, son enseignement, sa politique*, Paris, (Libraire Sandoz et Fischbacher), 1877.

De Ghellinck, J., "Un chapître dans l'histoire de la définition des sacraments au XIIe siècle," Mélanges Mandonnet, *Bibliothèque thomiste*, 14, (1930), 79-96.

De Lubac, H., *Corpus Mysticum, L'Eucharistie et L'Église au moyen-age*, Paris (Aubier), 1944.

Ebersolt, J., "Essai sur Bérenger de Tours et la controverse sacramentaire au XIe siècle," *Revue de l'histoire des Religions*, 48, (1903), pp. 1-42, 137-181.

Franzelin, J. Card., *Tractatus de ss. Eucharistiae, sacramento et sacrificio*, ed. 4ta, Rome, 1887.

Geiselmann, J., *Die Eucharistielehre der Vorscholastik*, Paderborn, (F. Schöningh), 1926.

Harnack, A., *History of Dogma*, vol. VI, transl. from 3rd German Ed., W. M'Gilchrist, London, 1899.

Héris, Ch. -V., O.P., *Le Mystère du Christ*, Paris, (Desclée), 1928.

Heurtevent, R., *Durand de Troarn et les origines de l'hérésie bérengerienne*, Paris, (Beauchesne), 1912.

Jansen, F., "Eucharistiques (accidents)," *DTC*, 5 (1913), 1368-1452.

Lecordier, G., *La doctrine de l'Eucharistie chez Saint Augustin*, Paris, (J. Gabalda), 1930.

Lepin, M., *L'Idee du Sacrifice de la Messe, d'aprés les théologiens, depuis l'origine jusquà nos jours*, 2nd Ed., Paris, (Beauchesne), 1926.

Masure, E., *The Christian Sacrifice*, trans. from 2nd Ed. of *Le Sacrifice du Chef*, (Beauchesne, Paris, 1932), with a preface by Dom Illtyd Trethowan, monk of Downside Abbey, London, (Burns, Oates, and Washbourne), 1944.

Macdonald, A. J., *Berengar and the Reform of Sacramental Doctrine*, London, (Longmans, Green and Co.), 1930.

———*Lanfranc, A Study of His Life, Work, and Writing*, London, (Society for Promoting Christian Knowledge), 1944.

Michel, A., "Sacrements," *DTC*, 14, (1939), 486-644.

Möhler, J. A., *Symbolism, or Exposition of the Doctrinal Differences between Catholics and Protestants*, ed. 5, (tr. by J. B. Robertson), London, 1906.

Morin, G., "Bérenger contre Bérenger," *Recherches de théologie ançienne et médiévale*, 4, (1932), 109-117.

Peltier, A., *Pascase Radbert, Abbé de Corbie*, Thèse pour le doctorat en théologie, Amiens, (L. H. Duthoit), 1938.

Pourrat, P., *Theology of the Sacraments*, authorized transl. from the 3rd French Ed., 2nd Ed., St. Louis, (B. Herder), 1914.

Redmond, R. P., "The Real Presence in the Early Middle Ages," *Clergy Review*, 8, (1934), 442-460.

Roach, W. J., "Eucharistic Tradition in the *Perlesvaus*," *Zeitschrift für Romanische Philologie*, 59, (1939), 10-56.

Sauvage, G., C.S.C., "Berengarius of Tours," *The Catholic Encyclopedia*, 2 (1907), 487-489.

Scheeben, M. J., *The Mysteries of Christianity*, (transl. C. Vollert, S.J.), St. Louis, (B. Herder),1946.

Schnitzer, J., *Berengar von Tours, sein Leben und seine Lehre*, (Stuttgart), 1892.

Stone, D., *A History of the Doctrine of the Holy Eucharist*, 2 vols., London, 1909.

———*The Holy Communion*, The Oxford Library of Practical Theology, London, 1904.

de la Taille, M., S.J., *Mysterium Fidei*, Ed. 2, Paris, (Beauchesne), 1924.

Turmel, J., *Histoire de la théologie positive, depuis l'origine jusqu' au Concile de Trent*, Ed. 3, Paris, 1904.

Vernet, F., "Bérenger de Tours," *DTC*, 2 (1905), 722-742.

———"Eucharistie du IXe siècle," *DTC*, 5: 1209-1233.

Vonier, A., *Sketches and Studies in Theology*, London, (Burns, Oates, and Washbourne), 1940.

INDEX OF SUBJECTS AND PROPER NAMES